UNITED NATIONS CONFERENCE ON TRADE AND DEVELOPMENT
Geneva

# Manual on trading
# with the socialist countries
# of Eastern Europe

## UNITED NATIONS
New York, 1985

**NOTE**

Symbols of United Nations documents are composed of capitals letters combined with figures. Mention of such a symbol indicates a reference to a United Nations document.

\* \*
\* \*

The designations employed and the presentation of the material in this publication do not imply the expression of any opinion whatsoever on the part of the Secretariat of the United Nations concerning the legal status of any country, territory, city or area, or of its authorities, or concerning the delimitation of its frontiers or boundaries.

\* \*
\* \*

UNCTAD/ST/TSC/1

UNITED NATIONS PUBLICATION

*Sales No.* E.85.II.D.10

ISBN 92-1-112198-1

01250P

## Introduction

The first edition of this Manual was brought out in 1983 within the framework of the UNDP/UNCTAD Comprehensive Programme of Technical Assistance for the Development of Trade between Developing Countries and Socialist Countries of Eastern Europe.  Taking into account the successful implementation of this Programme and pursuant to Trade and Development Board decisions, UNCTAD has continued this Programme of technical assistance which has, in fact, emerged as an important and major activity of UNCTAD in recent years.  This Programme covers training activities, dissemination of information and advisory services.  It has helped to equip officials and representatives of the business sector with the know-how needed for the task of identifying and exploring the potential for mutually beneficial trade relations with socialist countries.

The present revised edition of the Manual contains up-to-date information on the Council for Mutual Economic Assistance (CMEA) and the foreign trade systems, institutions, legal instruments, intergovernmental trade agreements, payments arrangements, economic co-operation agreements, modalities of trading, etc., of socialist countries of Eastern Europe.  The Manual is the first attempt of its kind in this field and the contents are by no means exhaustive.  Moreover, its limited size has precluded coverage of the various issues;  in greater depth.  For detailed information it would be necessary to refer to the various studies published by UNCTAD and the CMEA secretariat, as well as national publications on trade and economic co-operation among countries having different social and economic systems.

It is hoped that the Manual will provide some practical hints to the interested parties and that it will also be useful to the foreign trade institutions and business communities - especially those not already well acquainted with these countries - to help identify trade opportunities and to expand commercial contacts with the socialist countries of Eastern Europe.

Alister McIntyre
Deputy Secretary-General
Officer-in-Charge of UNCTAD

CONTENTS

|  |  | Page |
|---|---|---|
| | Introduction ........................................ | iii |
| Chapter I | The socialist countries of Eastern Europe and the Council for Mutual Economic Assistance (CMEA) ....... | 1 |
| Chapter II | The foreign trade system and institutions of the socialist countries of Eastern Europe .............. | 7 |
| Chapter III | Instruments for trade and economic co-operation ..... | 12 |
| Chapter IV | Marketing information ................................ | 17 |
| Chapter V | Trading with the USSR ................................ | 20 |
| Chapter VI | Trading with Bulgaria ............................... | 40 |
| Chapter VII | Trading with Czechoslovakia ......................... | 53 |
| Chapter VIII | Trading with the German Democratic Republic ......... | 66 |
| Chapter IX | Trading with Hungary ................................ | 78 |
| Chapter X | Trading with Poland ................................. | 93 |

Annex

| | List of some commercial publications of the socialist countries of Eastern Europe.......................... | 105 |

CONTENTS

## CHAPTER I

## THE SOCIALIST COUNTRIES OF EASTERN EUROPE AND THE
## COUNCIL FOR MUTUAL ECONOMIC ASSISTANCE (CMEA)

The socialist countries of Eastern Europe, after planned economic development during the last three decades, have assumed an important role on the world economic scene and in the field of international trade and economic relations. They now constitute about 9 per cent of world population (374 million) and their share of total world national income exceeds 25 per cent. They also account for approximately one-third of world industrial output and produce about 33 per cent of engineering and chemical hardware, 27 per cent of natural gas, 26 per cent of cement, 23 per cent of steel, 21 per cent of electricity and 19 per cent of crude oil.

The Council for Mutual Economic Assistance (CMEA) is an international organization of the socialist countries for promoting economic integration among member countries. Intra-CMEA trade and co-operation is conducted on the basis of the international division of labour according to equality, sovereignty and mutual benefits. The Council has contributed in no small measure to the speedy and planned development of the national economies of the socialist countries of Eastern Europe by uniting and co-ordinating the efforts of the member countries, as well as organizing their multilateral co-operation. CMEA was established in 1949 following an economic conference of representatives of Bulgaria, Czechoslovakia, Hungary, Poland, Romania and the Soviet Union. The German Democratic Republic joined in 1950, Mongolia in 1962, Cuba in 1972 and Viet Nam in 1978.

The charter of the Council says that its purpose is to promote, by uniting and co-ordinating the efforts of the member countries of the Council, the further extension and improvement of co-operation and the development of socialist economic integration, the planned and balanced development of national economies, the acceleration of economic and technological progress, a higher level of industrialization in the less industrialized member countries, a continuous increase in labour productivity, a gradual equalization of economic development levels, and a steady improvement in the well-being of the peoples of all member countries.

The Comprehensive Programme for the Further Extension and Improvement of Co-operation and the Development of Socialist Economic Integration of the CMEA Member Countries, adopted at the Council's twenty-fifth session in 1971, determines the basic directions of CMEA activities. The Comprehensive Programme is designed for stage-by-stage implementation over 15 to 20 years. Its aims are to promote, inter alia: 1/

(a) More rapid development of productive forces in all CMEA member countries, achievement of the highest scientific and technological levels and the maximum increase in the economic effectiveness of social production, as well as maximum growth in the productivity of social labour;

---

1/ See Comprehensive Programme for the Further Extension and Improvement of Co-operation and the Development of Socialist Economic Integration of the CMEA Member Countries (Moscow: CMEA, 1971).

(b)  The long-term satisfaction of countries' national economic requirement for fuel, power and raw materials, modern equipment, agricultural and food products, and other consumer goods, mainly through production and rational utilization of member countries' resources;

(c)  Gradual equalization of the economic development levels of member countries;

(d)  An increase in the material and cultural levels of the peoples of member countries;

(e)  Growth in the capacity and stability of the socialist world market; and

(f)  Strengthening of the positions of member countries in the world economy.

Provisions are made for the following main ways and means of attaining these goals:

(a)  Organizing multilateral and bilateral consultations among member countries on basic issues of economic policy;

(b)  Intensifying multilateral and bilateral co-operation in the planning activities of countries, including co-operation in forecasting, co-ordination of five-year and long-term plans for key branches of the economy and lines of production, joint planning by interested countries in agreed branches of industry, and exchange of experience with a view to improving the system of planning and economic management;

(c)  Systematic extension of international specialization and co-operation in the fields of production, science and technology, and the pooling of efforts by interested countries in mineral prospecting and mining, construction of industrial projects and research;

(d)  Systematic expansion in the effectiveness of mutual trade, and the improvement of its organizational forms on the basis of State monopoly;

(e)  Improvement of monetary and financial relations and the system of foreign trade prices;

(f)  Extension of direct links between ministries and other State bodies, economic, research and design organizations of CMEA member countries;

(g)  Development of existing international economic organizations and the creation of new ones by interested countries; and

(h)  Improvement of the legal basis of economic, scientific and technological co-operation, particularly with a view to increasing the material responsibility of each partner for non-fulfilment or inadequate fulfilment of mutual commitments.

## INTRA-CMEA CO-OPERATION

These countries have certain basic features that distinguish them from the developed market-economy countries. The following are the main characteristics:

(a) public ownership of means of production is universal;

(b) the economy is guided by over-all short-, medium- and long-term plans; and

(c) foreign trade and foreign exchange operations are a State monopoly and are regulated by the State.

Intra-CMEA co-operation in planning is intended to produce forecasts in the key fields of economy, science and technology; further improvement of co-ordination of five-year national economic plans; joint planning by interested countries of individual industrial branches and lines of production; and exchange of experience for improving the system of planning and national economic management.

Notable examples of the close co-operation among member countries in various fields of production, science and technology are: the long-distance intra-country oil and gas pipelines; the unified national power systems of the European CMEA member countries; the development and production of computers; co-operation in transport and common railway wagon pool set up by them; the joint construction of pulp production and asbestos extraction plants in the USSR; the copper and molybdenum concentrates works in Mongolia; the nickel-producing plants in Cuba; and the planned programme of nuclear power plant construction in the European CMEA member countries and Cuba, with a total capacity of 37 million kW.

## INTRA-CMEA TRADE

The development of trade between CMEA member countries is based on co-ordination of national economic plans. The five-year trade agreements, annual protocols and contracts stipulate the composition and volume of trade and indicate the terms of settlement of balances, either through bilateral balancing or by multilateral adjustments through the International Bank for Economic Co-operation (IBEC).

## INTRA-CMEA CO-OPERATION IN MONETARY, FINANCIAL AND CREDIT RELATIONS

Intra-CMEA co-operation in the monetary field is conducted through the International Bank for Economic Co-operation (IBEC) and the International Investment Bank (IIB).

IBEC started operations on 1 January 1964. Its major functions are to conclude international payments agreements; to undertake multilateral settlements in transferable roubles (the collective currency of CMEA member countries); to advance short and medium-term credits for financing foreign trade and other operation of member countries; to attract and keep non-commited funds in transferable roubles, gold, freely convertible and other currencies from member countries and from other countries; and to perform other banking operations corresponding to the aims and tasks specified in its statutes.

The authorized capital of IBEC is established at 304.4 million transferable roubles. The subscription quotas of member countries in this capital are determined in proportion to the specific weight of each country's export volume in total mutual trade. In 1981 the total volume of IBEC operations amounted to 208.4 billion transferable roubles, with mutual settlements of member countries effected through the bank totalling 140.2 billion transferable roubles.

IIB, established in 1971, is a credit institution for member countries granting long-term and medium-term credits for their capital investments, and above all for projects linked to their integrated economic co-operation. IIB may attract funds in transferable roubles, in national currencies of the countries concerned, and in convertible currencies by raising credits and loans, accepting deposits and by other means; place temporarily free funds with other banks, sell and buy currencies, gold and securities; and perform other banking operations in accordance with its statutes. Between 1971 and 1981, IIB extended credits worth 3.5 billion transferable roubles to finance about 80 large-scale projects.

The highest authorities in IBEC and IIB are their Councils, which consist of the representatives of each member country. Each member country, irrespective of the amount of its quota in the authorized capital, has one vote in the Councils. Decisions of the Council of each bank have to be adopted unanimously.

## SPECIALIZED INTERNATIONAL ORGANIZATIONS OF THE CMEA

CMEA member countries have established about 20 specialized international organizations for individual sectors and subsectors and types of production. These organizations constitute a major instrument of economic co-operation. In industry there is the Central Despatching Board (CDB) for the Unified Power System (the MIR energy system), the Organization for Co-operation in the Bearings Industry (OCBI), the Organization for Co-operation in the Iron and Steel Industry (Intermetal), the International Sectoral Organization for Co-operation in the Field of Small-Tonnage Chemical Products (Interchim) and the International Company for Machines for Vegetable Cultivation, Horticulture and Viticulture (Agromach). Other organizations are the International Centre for Economic, Scientific and Technological Co-operation in Electric Engineering (Interelectro); the Intergovernmental Commission on Co-operation of Socialist Countries in the Field of Computing Technology; a number of organizations in transport and communications; the Railway Wagon Pool (RWP); the Board of the Organization for Joint Container Utilization; the International Shipowners Association (ISA); and the International System and Space Communications Organization (Intersputnik).

## CMEA AND NON-MEMBER COUNTRIES

CMEA has also concluded co-operation agreements with non-member countries. On the basis of a 1964 co-operation agreement, Yugoslavia is participating in 23 areas of activity of the Council, including CMEA bodies dealing with foreign trade, monetary and financial relation, scientific and technological co-operation, ferrous and non-ferrous metallurgy, engineering, etc.

According to the Co-operation Agreement between CMEA and Finland 1973, 22 multilateral and bilateral agreements have been concluded on economic, industrial, scientific and technological co-operation. They cover engineering, a comprehensive use of timber, raw materials, oil, gas, environmental protection and transport.

In 1975 agreements on co-operation with CMEA were concluded by Iraq and Mexico. Within the joint commission of CMEA and Iraq there are working groups on the oil and gas industries, agriculture and irrigation, scientific and technological co-operation, foreign trade and freight transport. The Mixed Commission on Co-operation of CMEA and Mexico has set up working groups on scientific and technological co-operation and fisheries, as well as a conference of experts on foreign trade to seek out opportunities for increasing the commodity turnover between CMEA member countries and Mexico.

Afghanistan, Angola, Ethiopia, the Lao People's Democratic Republic, Mozambique and Democratic Yemen participate in CMEA sessions as observers.

## TRADE WITH DEVELOPING COUNTRIES

In 1982, the volume of trade between the socialist countries of Eastern Europe and developing countries was 64.6 billion dollars, compared with 2.8 billion dollars in 1960 (see table 1). Over this period, the annual rate of growth in the volume of trade between the two groups of countries averaged about 14 per cent.

### Table 1

### Volume of foreign trade of European CMEA member countries with developing countries

(billion dollars)

|                          | 1960 | 1970 | 1975 | 1980 | 1982 |
|--------------------------|------|------|------|------|------|
| Turnover<br>of which:    | 2.8  | 9.3  | 25.7 | 55.9 | 64.6 |
| exports                  | 1.3  | 5.5  | 13.7 | 30.2 | 37.5 |
| imports                  | 1.5  | 3.8  | 12.0 | 25.7 | 27.1 |

Source: UNCTAD secretariat.

The expansion of trade relations with the developing countries has led to an increase in their share of the socialist countries' trade turnover (from 6.9 per cent in 1960 to 22.6 per cent in 1982), with a stable tendency towards growth. The socialist countries provide their trading partners in Africa, Asia and Latin America with machines, equipment and other industrial products (such as chemical products, fertilizers and building materials). They also export industrial consumer goods and food products, whose volume grows from year to year. At the same time, the share of consumer goods in the exports of the socialist countries is decreasing as the developing countries establish their own light and food industries.

Raw materials account for a major share of the socialist countries' imports from developing countries (about half the total imports). Citrus fruits, coffee, cocoa, bananas, natural rubber, cotton fibres and other products from tropical and subtropical zones account for an important share of these goods. Although the proportion of these products in the socialist countries' total imports is declining somewhat their supply increased more than six-fold towards the end of the 1970s compared with 1960. The import structure has undergone significant changes resulting from increased purchases by the socialist countries of fuel, minerals and metals from developing countries. By the end of the 1970s, these products accounted for two-fifths of the value of their imports from the developing countries.

The socialist countries of Eastern Europe attach priority to increasing each year their purchases of manufactures and semi-manufactures from the developing countries, thus contributing to the development of the national economies of the developing countries.

## CHAPTER II

## THE FOREIGN TRADE SYSTEM AND INSTITUTIONS OF THE SOCIALIST COUNTRIES OF EASTERN EUROPE

The foreign trade policy of the socialist countries of Eastern Europe is an inseparable part of their general economic policy, the principal aim of which is to intensify the involvement of the national economies in the international division of labour.

Foreign trade is a State monopoly in all socialist countries, operating through a host of State-run organizations which fall clearly into two types: those relating to general administration and guidance, and those that deal with imports and exports. 1/

### ORGANIZATION OF FOREIGN TRADE

The central government organ for control, administration and guidance of foreign trade affairs is the Ministry of Foreign Trade (in some countries it has a different name, but its functions are the same). Its duties and responsibilities ensue from the planned nature of socialist economies. Foreign trade and other forms of external economic activity are undertaken on the basis of State monopoly. In the USSR, the direction, co-ordination and control of activities for organizing economic and technical co-operation with foreign countries are carried out by the State Committee for External Economic Relations. 2/

The structure of the Ministry of Foreign Trade in various socialist countries is basically the same. There are trade policy (regional), commodity (sectoral) and functional directorates and departments. Each Ministry of Foreign Trade elaborates the fundamentals of national trade policy, works out foreign trade plans and supervises their implementation, conducts intergovernmental negotiations to conclude agreements and treaties and exercises control over their implementation, and makes recommendations concerning the maintenance and expansion of trade relations with particular countries. The Ministry of Foreign Trade ensures that all foreign trade institutions in the country adhere to the national policy of the State. International agreements on specialization and co-operation in production, and on financial, credit, transport and other matters may be concluded by other ministries and departments with the approval of the Ministry of Foreign Trade.

Trade policy work in the Ministry of Foreign Trade is carried out by departments and directorates responsible for trade (or economic) relations with particular regions and countries. As a rule, these departments fall into two large groups: those dealing with trade with the socialist countries, and those concerned with other countries.

In some socialist countries, the Ministries of Foreign Trade have recently adopted a new approach to planning and set up special division for long-term

---

1/ For details, see chapters V-X.

2/ For details of the functions of the Committee, see chapter V.

planning, scientific forecasting, etc. Thus the Ministry of Foreign Economic Relations of the German Democratic Republic has, in addition to its planning directorate, a Department of Long-Term and Annual Planning, a Department of Foreign Exchange Planning and a Department of Forecasts and Structural Policy.

The Ministries of Foreign Trade in socialist countries are now allowing foreign trade organizations more flexibility in the fulfilment of plans and other areas of decision making. The foreign trade organizations are now subject to less binding indicators in their plans and are given more rights to independent decision making.

## FOREIGN TRADE PLANNING

Under the system of foreign trade monopoly, the basic element in the regulation of foreign trade is the plan, which is growth oriented and is the main instrument of trade policy. It is aimed at expanding international co-operation and thereby also foreign trade, in accordance with the needs and potential of the national economy. A national foreign trade plan is compiled in terms of the value of foreign currencies and, in some cases, in terms of quantity. The plan in terms of value embraces most of the future export and import deliveries. It also contains details of design and civil engineering works and cost estimates for services.

The foreign trade plan, as an integral part of the national economic plan, has binding force and provides a foundation for the relevant plans of the Ministry of Foreign Trade, foreign trade enterprises and other industries concerned. Foreign trade planning is based on forecasting the tendencies expected in world markets and is interlinked with the development of all sectors of the national economy. It is compiled for a period of five years, with subsequent elaboration of short-term annual plans. Export and import plans fully reflect the commitments envisaged in international trade agreements. The endorsement of the plan is within the competence of the government of the respective socialist State.

An important feature of foreign trade planning, just as of other sectors of the national economy, is that export and import projections must conform to the balance of resources and requirements. The plan assignments are worked out in detail by the Ministry of Foreign Trade. The general export assignments for particular products for export are estimated in terms of cost value at domestic and foreign trade prices. Deliveries of the most important goods forming part of the general assignment are estimated in terms of quantity and have binding force for producers. Import assignments are estimated in a similar way. Integral parts of the foreign trade plan are the foreign currency plan and the estimated balance of payment, whose indicators are binding.

The performance of foreign trade enterprises is supervised by the Ministry of Foreign Trade through regular progress reports submitted by the former containing complete information on the extent to which the performance of the respective foreign trade enterprise is in conformity with plan targets for exports and imports.

To couple centralized management of external economic activities with the growing initiative of associations, combines, enterprises and foreign trade organizations, the CMEA member countries have in the past few years introduced substantial changes in the nature and content of their plans for external economic relations. In particular, they have sharply reduced the number of plan targets, reduced and generalized assignments for a variety of exported products, increased the number and extended the meaning of cost indicators in order to adjust planning both to the changing conditions of foreign markets and the need for planned conduct of external activities. Such measures have contributed to the growth of independent action by enterprises.

The impact of medium-term (five-year) and annual plans on economic relations with foreign countries varies from country to country. In some States, such as Czechoslovakia and Poland, enterprises depend on annual plans only. CMEA member countries also exhibit differences between the centralized planning of foreign economic relations and their planning at national enterprise level, each varying in degree and scope. One thing makes this sphere of planning different from all the others: estimates are increasingly made in terms of value, because balances of payments and foreign currency revenues must be brought into equilibrium.

Industrial complexes, associations and enterprises increasingly play a major part in the planning of foreign economic relations. They have substantial rights to act on their own when planning and producing export merchandise. They have complete freedom in selecting export items within the value limits for each commodity group established by State planning agencies and sectoral ministries.

The nature of the economic plans of different socialist countries varies substantially. For example, in Hungary, while the national economic plan determines the general guidelines of the economic activity, the main central economic policy targets, including those connected with the foreign trade, are transmitted to the enterprises through economic regulators, mainly by the price system, the exchange rate policy, and by other monetary and fiscal measures. Those are the only instruments of the authorities to influence and orientate the enterprises activities. 1/

## TRADE REPRESENTATION ABROAD

Offices of trade representatives/commercial counsellors are part of the diplomatic missions of CMEA member countries. They represent their country's interests in foreign trade, promote the development of trade and economic relations with the host country and monitor foreign trade exchanges with that country.

In accordance with their duties, trade representatives might be authorized to conclude foreign trade transactions for their countries' organizations and enterprises and ensure that foreign trade laws and instructions of their governments are observed by organizations involved in foreign trade. The representatives of foreign trade enterprises that have established close business relations with the respective host country are also appointed in the trade representations to handle import and export operations.

In some countries where the socialist countries do not have an agreement for a trade representation, there are commercial counsellors' offices attached to embassies, whose activities are similar to those of trade representatives. When rendering technical assistance in the construction of industrial enterprises and

---

1/ For the different details see chapter V-X.

other projects in foreign countries, some socialist States are represented by
their economic counsellors' offices.  In the case of the USSR, these offices work
under the guidance of the State Committee for External Economic Relations.  The
Office of Economic Counsellor ensures the interests and rights of its country in
the field of economic co-operation and technical assistance in the construction
of complete plants and other projects, as well as in the training of national
manpower.  It elaborates proposals for developing economic ties with the country
in question.  It organizes and supervises work by groups of experts coming to
prepare feasibility studies, and ensures that contractors from its home country
meet their commitments in rendering technical assistance.

## FOREIGN TRADE ORGANIZATIONS (FTOs)

The structure of foreign trade machinery in the socialist countries depends
on the social and economic tasks the particular country has to undertake.  A
major task in this field is to ensure the maximum possible co-operation between
those involved in foreign trade and industry, and to stimulate producers' interest
in all foreign commercial transactions.

Closer links between industry and foreign trade have been achieved by
different methods in different socialist countries, yet efforts have clearly
been exerted in two major directions that explain the present structure of
foreign trade institutions:

(a)  close links between producers and foreign trade institutions, and
mutual responsibility for the results of commercial deals; and

(b)  direct involvement (in various forms) of industrial enterprises in
commercial deals.

A tendency has been observed in nearly all the socialist countries for the
number of FTOs to increase, triggered by a more profound specialization, in
particular commodities or products, and by the need to perform different
functions to ensure the expansion of foreign trade.  In spite of the multiple
forms of foreign trade organizations vested with powers to operate in foreign
markets, they fall into four major groups:

(a)  specialized FTOs;

(b)  FTOs or their independent offices incorporated into industrial
associations;

(c)  industrial enterprises with the right of direct access to foreign
markets; and

(d)  foreign trade co-operative organizations.

The operative economic machinery of the socialist countries' foreign trade
is mostly represented by specialized FTOs, which usually carry out trade in
certain commodity groups.  Until recently, specialized FTOs were the only export-
and import-oriented institutions.  FTOs are independent, self-supporting
establishments dealing in a limited variety of goods at their own expense.  They
are responsible for the deals they make and the State bears no responsibility for
their transactions or any commitments by them.

A specialized department (in the case of a Soviet FTO, a specialized form)
is a major subdivision of all modern foreign trade establishments.  The present

tendency is to make each department (firm) and, indeed, the FTO as a whole operates on a profit-and-loss basis. The reorganization of foreign trade establishments that has been under way for the past few years has left intact their commodity-orientation or regional principle of organization.

Foreign trade establishments of the socialist countries of Eastern Europe have set up mixed companies in some developed market-economy countries, in which they control the bulk of share capital. Such mixed companies usually engage in brokerage while studying demand, promoting sales, providing technical maintenance, etc. Mixed companies are increasingly used by Bulgaria, Czechoslovakia, the German Democratic Republic and Poland.

There are various forms of co-operation between industry and foreign trade establishments in the socialist countries. In Hungary, FTOs involve the so-called councils of directors of the respective industries in their work. The above auxiliary units have a deliberative vote and are obliged to co-ordinate foreign trade activities with those of industrial producers.

In the German Democratic Republic, Czechoslovakia and Hungary, industrial enterprises increasingly take part in advertising the goods they want to export.

## CHAMBERS OF COMMERCE

Chambers of commerce are non-governmental organizations whose members are foreign trade organizations, industrial and commercial institutions, etc. They have numerous responsibilities. They promote domestic trade and foreign economic relations, provide information to foreign firms and national organizations with a view to establishing businees contacts and finding additional markets, establish relations with foreign industrial and commercial organizations and international organizations, and generally promote international economic co-operation. They arrange business visits by foreign commercial and industrial delegations, as well as foreign visits by national delegations to investigate foreign markets. A very important responsibility of the chambers is to arrange international trade fairs and exhibitions. They also deal with the foreign trade documents and certificates necessary for international business contacts. They have commissions and bureaux of experts to check the quality of goods, and arbitration commissions to settle trade disputes with foreign trading partners.

The chambers of commerce and industry of the CMEA member countries take part in international congresses of chambers of commerce and establish joint (or mixed) chambers of commerce with their counterparts in other countries.

CHAPTER III

INSTRUMENTS FOR TRADE AND ECONOMIC CO-OPERATION

During the 1970s, both the socialist countries of Eastern Europe and the majority of developing countries became increasingly aware that the possibilities of promoting mutually beneficial trade relations depended on a further development of an integrated complex of measures, including - in addition to traditional methods and instruments of trade policy - various other aspects of international economic relations, such as economic and technical assistance, industrial ventures, transfer of technology, etc.   To an ever-increasing extent, trade is fostered by a desire on both sides to create new trading opportunities and promote a new structure of exchange through a series of practical measures for directly or indirectly improving the economic basis of trade flows.

I.  BILATERAL FORMS OF CO-OPERATION

A.  Intergovernmental Treaties and Agreements

The basic documents regulating trade and economic relations between the socialist countries and other States are long-term trade treaties (or trade and maritime treaties) and agreements.

Long-term agreements are one of the major instruments for facilitating trade between the socialist countries of Eastern Europe and the developing countries.   They perform multiple functions, including the establishment of general trade policy conditions, the harmonization of export and import policies, trade promotion, and so on.   They also make it possible to relate expansion of trade to developments in other areas of co-operation and to the economic plans and programmes in partner countries.

Generally the treaties and agreements incorporate the basic principle of international trade - the principle of most-favoured-nation (MFN) treatment. Commercial relations among CMEA member countries are based on five-year agreements on the mutual delivery of goods, which reflect the results of concerted efforts to co-ordinate national economic plans.   Long-term trade agreements are implemented through annual protocols on mutual delivery of goods which specify the volume/value of goods stipulated by these agreements for the respective year.

Foreign trade and other economic relations between the Soviet Union, other socialist countries and non-socialist States are regulated above all, by trade and payments agreements between the governments of the respective countries. Moreover, some intergovernmental agreements (protocols) on the delivery of machinery and equipment also stipulate certain specific terms of repayment. A number of developing countries have regulations specifying that, for the import of machinery and equipment, the suppliers should offer credits on deferred payment terms.

Co-operation based on long-term intergovernmental agreements is increasing year by year.   It enables the contracting countries to plan their economic development with long-term perspective.   CMEA member countries have concluded such long-term agreements with many developing States.

A noticeable trend in trade relations between the socialist countries of Eastern Europe and developing countries in recent years has been the extended duration of intergovernmental agreements (up to 10 or 15 years) and their gradual transformation into comprehensive co-operation programmes, simultaneously regulating and co-ordinating economic, industrial, scientific and technological relations between the contracting parties. These agreements have been concluded between the USSR and India (10 to 15 years), Poland and the Islamic Republic of Iran (15 years), and Bulgaria and the Islamic Republic of Iran (15 years).

Mutual business-like co-operation is also promoted by joint intergovernmental commissions. The joint commissions undertake to check on the progress of implementation of agreements on trade, economic, scientific and technical co-operation, to review all possibilities, and to elaborate and consider proposals for the further development of bilateral co-operation. These activities offer new opportunities for expanding and diversifying foreign economic ties between the partners.

## B. Payments Arrangements

Payments clauses constitute an integral part of trade agreements. The form of payment is determined by agreement between the parties, with consideration being given to various factors affecting the trade and economic relations of the respective socialist country of Eastern Europe with a particular developing country.

For many years, clearing arrangements were the predominant form of payment and this practice helped to establish and expand trade relations between the socialist countries of Eastern Europe and the developing countries, especially in the initial periods. During the 1970s, however, many of these clearing agreements were replaced by new agreements stipulating payments in convertible currencies. For example, by early 1982 only six countries, namely Afghanistan, Egypt, India, the Islamic Republic of Iran, Pakistan and the Syrian Arab Republic, had retained clearing system arrangements in their bilateral trade with the USSR. A similar pattern may be observed in payments relations between other socialist countries and developing countries.

## C. Economic Co-operation

Agreements on economic co-operation between the socialist countries of Eastern Europe and the developing countries are relatively new, compared with trade agreements, and reflect the partner countries' desire to deepen their relations on a long-term (10-15 years) and stable basis. These agreements usually cover the following fields:

(a) Trade related to projects under the agreements, including marketing and after-sales services;

(b) Economic co-operation to set up new production capacities and expand and modernize existing capacities in developing countries, to develop natural resources, and to develop or improve infrastructure;

(c) Co-operation in production through subcontracting, joint assembling and other means of joint production;

(d)  Scientific and technical co-operation between enterprises and scientific institutions;

(e)  Co-operation in planning;  and

(f)  Co-operation in third countries, etc.

Socialist countries base their co-operation with other countries both on the requirements of their partners and on mutual benefits.  The first step in any scheme of industrial co-operation is to analyse the technical and economic conditions and possible effects of such a project.

## D.  Industrial Co-operation

In recent years, and particularly during the 1970s, industrial co-operation (especially between the socialist countries of Eastern Europe and more advanced developing countries) has evolved to take on more sophisticated forms, including specialization and co-operation on the basis of a long-term harmonization of the partners' investment, production and technological cycles.  Thus the development of industrial co-operation, mostly within the framework of long-term intergovernmental agreements, contributes to a stable exchange of manufactured and semi-manufactured products.  An increasing role is played by the supply of complete plants and equipment to developing countries.  At the end of 1981, 79.4 per cent of all the projects of the socialist countries in developing countries were carried out in the industry and energy sectors, while the rest were distributed as follows:  agriculture (5.0 per cent), transportation and communications (5.4 per cent), geological prospecting (4.9 per cent), health education, utilities and others (5.3 per cent).

A promising form of economic co-operation between the CMEA member countries and the developing nations is co-operation on the basis of compensatory agreements (buy-back deals).  Buy-back projects have enabled the developing countries to launch new export-oriented industries and, in so doing, enhance their capacity to buy more machines and equipment and other indispensable goods, as well as to reimburse technical services.  Co-operation on a compensatory basis plays an important part in expanding exports from developing countries to European CMEA member countries, not only of raw materials, but of processed and manufactured products as well.  Buy-back deals allow CMEA member countries to expand their mutually beneficial commercial and economic ties with a number of developing countries on a long-term basis, as well as enabling them to plan their import requirements over the long term.

## E.  Joint Manufacture of Goods

In recent years, industrial joint ventures have become increasingly popular.  There are about 100 mixed companies in which CMEA member countries are involved in the developing countries.  These companies operate in accordance with the laws of the respective developing countries, including regulations on the size of a host country's share in the joint capital.  One important point about these companies is that the developing host country has the right to buy out the share of a socialist country in the joint capital if it so desires, and thereafter to become a full owner of the company and the project it has built.  Socialist countries' foreign trade organizations are members of joint stock companies operating in various sectors of the developing countries.

On the whole, industrial joint ventures ensure a transfer of technology and know-how and help developing countries to export their non-traditional goods to the CMEA member countries.

## II. MULTILATERAL FORMS OF CO-OPERATION

Both public and private enterprises in the developing countries can participate in the implementation of various projects carried out within the framework of socialist economic integration. The decisions of recent CMEA sessions envisage a concentration of efforts by all member States on implementing long-term specific co-operation programmes in such vital spheres of production as: fuel, power and raw materials; agriculture and the food industry; machine building; production of industrial consumer goods; and transport and communications.

The most developed form of multilateral relations between the two groups of countries is tripartite co-operation involving more than one socialist country in providing assistance to the developing countries. Such co-operation covers some 200 projects in developing countries. For example, economic organizations of Czechoslovakia and the German Democratic Republic participate, on a co-operative basis, in the design and delivery of certain types of equipment for the metallurgical works under construction in India, Pakistan and Turkey (with the technical assistance of the Soviet Union), within the framework of specialization and co-production established among CMEA member countries. The construction of cement plants in the Syrian Arab Republic with an aggregate annual capacity of 1.3 million tons (with the assistance of the German Democratic Republic) involved the delivery of certain types of technological equipment from Czechoslovakia and the USSR, while the installation operations were carried out with the participation of experts from Bulgaria.

Joint efforts by CMEA member countries' organizations and those of developing countries in third countries' markets or in rendering assistance to another developing country constitute a new form of co-operation. Thus the USSR has placed orders for Indian-made equipment to be delivered to third countries where it is engaged in building industrial enterprises, (e.g. in Nigeria, Algeria and Turkey). Czechoslovak organizations co-operate with companies in India and Iraq in carrying out various projects in the developing countries. Other examples include co-operation by Indian firms with Hungarian organizations in building light-bulb plants in the Philippines, Indonesia and Sri Lanka, and with Czechoslovak organization in the construction of a motorcycle assembly plant in the Islamic Republic of Iran.

### INTERGOVERNMENTAL CREDITS

Government credits are granted within the framework of intergovernmental agreements on economic co-operation. To implement these agreements, the State banks of the socialist countries act as their governments' intermediaries in the banking procedures. Since these credits are of an intergovernmental character, their terms and conditions are specific and of a long-term nature, with low interest rates. Repayment of such credits usually begins either when complete sets of plants have been delivered; or when a project has been commissioned and begins to yield sizeable profits to the debtor country.

Bilateral intergovernmental agreements and programmes on economic co-operation with developing countries usually contain long-term credit arrangements which are an integral part of them and provide for the financing of the projects concerned. In cases of economic and technical co-operation, priority is given to intergovernmental long-term credits for a period of 10-15 years, with a relatively long grace period and 2.5-3.0 per cent interest. Recently, due to a substantial rise in the interest rates in world capital markets, a certain part of such credits has been granted to developing countries at a 3-4 per cent interest rate. Some State credits are granted for a period of 25-30 years.

Credits granted to developing countries are repaid by them, as a rule, in traditional export goods. In some cases, credits may be repaid in goods produced by enterprises built in co-operation with a particular socialist country. Goods are exported in repayment of credits in accordance with trade agreements concluded between a CMEA member country and the respective developing country.

The Soviet Union and other socialist countries grant government credits under agreement with the governments of the developing countries concerned. These credits are intended, above all, for the construction of industrial projects, designing, delivery, erection and installation of machinery and equipment, training of national manpower, etc. It should be noted that such credits do not cover the over-all costs of projects, and thus the balance is to be paid by the respective country (for the construction of premises, access ways, auxiliary structures, etc. - i.e. local costs).

## BANK CREDITS

Credits are granted to the developing countries by the specialized banks of the socialist countries in the form of commercial and bank credits. The granting of credits to promote mutual trade grew fast in the 1960s, and particularly in the 1970s. Banks of the socialist countries concluded credit agreements with the central banks of the developing countries or with commercial banks acting on behalf of these central banks, or with their national financial development institutions. The specific features of bank crediting are its goal-oriented nature and the equality of partners. A bank credit is usually granted for a period of 2-3 years with a clause stipulating the possibility of extension. As regards the rate of interest on such credits, the CMEA member countries' banks take into account existing world money market rates; but bank credit rates are, in fact, usually lower than the average world rates or those on commercial credits.

## COMMERCIAL CREDITS

Another form of crediting is the granting of commercial credits by foreign trade organizations of the CMEA member countries directly to their foreign counterparts. In such cases, periods of redemption may differ depending on the type of merchandise, while rates of interest normally follow the world average. For example, Soviet foreign trade organizations extend commercial credits for a fixed term of up to five years. In the case of deliveries on commercial terms of heavy machinery and equipment, longer terms of up to 10 years may be negotiated.

## CHAPTER IV

## MARKETING INFORMATION

For a successful access to the markets of the socialist countries of Eastern Europe, exporter from developing countries should systematically examine the "trade data", including data on production, foreign trade and planned targets and priorities, importing procedures and regulations, currency regulations, trade agreements, product specifications and quality grade, as well as the statutes of the FTOs and their organizational structure. This trade data can be obtained from various publications, international organizations, and governmental and private organizations outside CMEA member countries. However, not all the trade and market data an exporter needs can be found in published form. Detailed statistical data, official regulations on foreign trade and information on the institutional structure of external economic relations are usually published in the national language.

In these circumstances, a market survey will have to be conducted by sending official or business missions to the CMEA member countries, perhaps coinciding with international trade fairs or specialized exhibitions. When undertaking market surveys in the socialist countries, the specific features of their economies, including public ownership of the means of production, the planning system and the state monopoly in foreign trade should be taken into account. A developing country firm may also consult its country's commercial mission and offices of state-trading organizations, if any, in these countries to collect marketing information needed for promoting trade.

If an exporter from a developing country is new to these markets he should collect complete information in the following areas before he launches his marketing effort:

(a) Production and consumption targets. CMEA member countries run their economies on the basis of short-term and long-term goals. These goals are indicated in the annual and five-year plans. Careful study of current plans can help exporters to determine long-term import requirements of a target country. The five-year plans give a general outline of the targeted output and expansion of capacity for each industrial branch and services sector of the economy. The difference between targeted output during each year of the plan and targeted consumption during the same period is the major factor used in estimating the volume of imports. Long-term growth potential for imported goods can be estimated by a study of the previous and current five-year plans;

(b) Imports from other countries. Bilateral trade agreements provide for mutual deliveries of goods and services on a long-term basis. These agreements usually reflect long-standing commercial relations between the respective trading partners and their estimates of further mutual needs, rather than an administrative desire to promote such trade; and

(c) Product specifications. Once a developing country exporter has established the potential for his products in these markets, he must obtain data about quantities required, qualities/grades, prices currently paid, payment conditions, delivery times, etc., to enable him to make offers to the competent FTOs.

## PRINCIPAL SOURCES OF TRADE AND MARKET DATA

### A. PLANNING DOCUMENTS

FTOs and the enterprises authorized to handle foreign trade/transactions base their decisions to export and import largely on the priorities reflected in foreign trade plans, which are based on the five-year plan and the annual plan.

Five-year plans are available as published documents. Summaries of the annual plan are usually published before the plan year begins, giving the major targeted aggregates by economic and industrial sector. Performance in the various areas of the plan is reported after the beginning of the following year. These summaries are usually published in the major economic periodicals of the respective countries.

### B. TRADE DOCUMENTS

The bilateral trade agreements of the CMEA member countries and their foreign partners are published in a variety of publications, usually the official bulletins   the Ministr  s of Foreign Trade or the chambers of commerce. Lists of products to be traded under these agreements are specified in sufficient detail to help exporters dealing in the same goods to estimate the current import needs of the countries. In some cases, these lists specify the quantity of the value of the products to be traded.

### C. STATISTICAL SOURCES

Before making use of official trade statistics it is necessary to understand fully the Standard Foreign Trade Classification of the CMEA, since it differs substantially from the Standard International Trade Classification (SITC). The commodity classification used by CMEA member count  es for their foreign trade is based on end use, whereas the SITC is based on specific types of goods. The two systems of classifica  on can be matched, however, using the conversion key prepared by the secretariat of the Untied Nations Economic Commission for Europe (ECE) in co-operation with the CMEA secretariat. 1/

Chambers of commerce are one of the best sources of non-statistical data. Their publications give information on FTOs and enterprises engaged in foreign trade, indicating the products they handle.

The periodicals of the socialist countries of Eastern Europe, including economic, commercial, industrial, technical and specialized commercial publications, can be of great assistance to foreign exp  ters. While many of these reviews are usually published in the national language of each country, foreign trade bulletins and other specialized commercial periodicals are published in five major languages - English, French, German, Russian and Spanish. These

_____

1/ CES/AC.38/4, 12 July 1978, available in English and Russian.

periodicals are the main source of official data on production and consumption targets, production plans and planned priorities.  Articles based on interviews with leading ministry officials on the trade and production plans of particular industries or economic sectors are also published in the press.  Foreign trade bulletins and newsletters are an important source of news about recent trade agreement, visits of trade missions abroad, imports from Eastern European countries and new products offered for export.

A list of commercial publications of the socialist countries of Eastern Europe is given in the annex to this manual.

## CHAPTER V

## TRADING WITH THE USSR

## 1. ECONOMY

The Union of Soviet Socialist Republics (USSR or Soviet Union) is a multinational State of more than 100 nations and nationalities, uniting 15 Soviet socialist republics. It is also the world's largest country, covering an area of 22.4 million square kilometres - i.e., one sixth of the earth's surface. It has the third largest population in the world after China and India, comprising 271.2 million people in 1982.

In the USSR, the world's first socialist economy, the means of production are owned by the State and economic resources are allocated on the basis of co-ordinated economic plans.

### MINERAL RESOURCES

The USSR is self-sufficient in all major industrial minerals except bauxite tin and uranium. It is the largest producer of iron ore, manganese, chromium and tungsten in the world. It is the second largest producer of copper, lead, zinc, magnesium, cadmium and mercury, and the third largest producer of nickel and molybdenum. It is one of the most important producers of gold and precious metals, accounting for nearly 20 per cent of the world's production of silver, platinum and diamonds. The USSR is also one of the biggest producers and exporters of petroleum, its share in world production being about 14 per cent.

### AGRICULTURAL RESOURCES

The USSR has rich agricultural, forestry and fisheries resources. However, it also has certain handicaps such as widely differing conditions of soil, weather, etc. The USSR contains one third of the world's forests, mainly the vast coniferous forests of Siberia and the far-east region. While not yet fully exploited, the potential of these resources is very great.

### STRUCTURE OF THE ECONOMY

The Soviet Union possesses great economic, technical and scientific potential. The gross domestic product of the USSR amounted to 523.4 billion dollars in 1982. 1/ During the last two decades (1960-1981), the annual growth rates of the basic indicators characterizing the USSR's economic development were as follows: gross domestic product (GDP) and national income increased, on average, by 5.9 per cent, industrial production by 7.0 per cent, agricultural production by 2.0 per cent, capital investment by 5.9 per cent, retail trade turnover by 6.1 per cent and real income per capita by 4.3 per cent.

---

1/ UNCTAD Handbook of International Trade and Development Statistics: Supplement 1984 (United Nations publication, Sales No. E/F.84.II.D.12).

The Soviet Union accounts for more than 20 per cent of the world's industrial production. It produces daily 3.54 billion kilowatt-hours of electricity; 1.65 million tons of crude oil; 1.19 billion cubic metres of natural gas; 1.96 million tons of coal; 0.4 million tons of steel; 6,000 cars and trucks; 1,500 tractors; 342,000 tons of cement; and 29.3 million square metres of various fabrics. In 1980 the USSR ranked first in world production of crude oil, pig iron, steel, iron ore, coke, mineral fertilizers, cement woollen fabrics and leather footwear.

The eleventh National Five-Year Plan (1981-1985) aims at an annual economic growth of 3.4-3.7 per cent. Capital investment should increase each year, on the average, by 1.6 per cent; industrial production by 4.7-5.1 per cent; consumer goods production by 4.9-5.2 per cent; agricultural production by 2.3-2.7 per cent; and foreign trade by 4.1 per cent. Major industries being accorded high priority are fuel and electric power production, engineering and electrical engineering, electronics and computers, industrial robots, chemicals, synthetic resins and plastics, mineral fertilizers and agricultural production.

## II. FOREIGN TRADE OF THE USSR

Foreign trade and other external economic activities of the USSR are a State monopoly, a fact which determines the organizational structure of foreign trade. The role of foreign trade in the USSR, a large country with a diversified resource base, is not important quantitatively. However, its importance in the national income and in planning mechanism has grown over the years. Foreign trade is an additional instrument for accelerating growth and achieving higher production levels, raising labour efficiency and providing the fullest satisfaction of the working peoples' material and cultural requirements.

### DIRECTION OF TRADE

The rate of growth of the USSR's total foreign trade turnover for the period 1960-1981 was much higher (12.04 per cent) than the rates of growth of basic economic indicators given above. Trade and economic relations are maintained with 142 countries, including relations with 116 countries on the basis of intergovernmental agreements on trade and economic and industrial co-operation. While the major trading partners of the USSR remain the CMEA countries, followed by developed market-economy countries, the importance of trade with developing countries is steadily expanding as a matter of policy. Table 2 shows the geographical distribution of Soviet foreign trade.

As table 2 shows, the major trading partners of the USSR are the socialist countries of Eastern Europe, followed by the developed market-economy countries and the developing countries.

Table 2

Geographical distribution of
USSR foreign trade

(value in millions of dollars f.o.b.)

| | Exports | | | | Imports | | | |
|---|---|---|---|---|---|---|---|---|
| | 1960 | 1970 | 1980 | 1982 | 1960 | 1970 | 1980 | 1982 |
| Total | 5 564 | 12 800 | 76 492 | 86 968 | 5 628 | 11 732 | 68 522 | 77 668 |
| Socialist countries of Eastern Europe | 3 118 | 6 758 | 32 239 | 36 204 | 2 819 | 6 634 | 29 428 | 33 489 |
| Share in per cent | 56.0 | 52.8 | 42.1 | 41.6 | 50.1 | 56.5 | 42.9 | 43.1 |
| Developed market-economy countries | 1 023 | 2 456 | 24 953 | 26 162 | 1 121 | 2 852 | 24 404 | 26 143 |
| Share in per cent | 18.4 | 19.2 | 32.6 | 30.1 | 19.9 | 24.3 | 35.6 | 33.7 |
| Developing countries a/ | 606 | 3 561 | 19 039 | 24 436 | 840 | 2 224 | 14 464 | 17 894 |
| Share in per cent | 10.9 | 27.8 | 24.9 | 28.1 | 14.9 | 19.0 | 21.1 | 23.0 |

Source: UNCTAD, "Trends and policies in trade and economic co-operation among countries having different economic and social systems: Statistical annex" (TD/B/1003/Add.1).

a/ Excluding China.

## COMPOSITION OF TRADE

The export commodity structure for the period 1970-1982 reveals an increase (from 45.1 per cent to 52.3 per cent), in value terms, in the share of fuel/energy, with a decline in the share of machinery and equipment (from 21.5 per cent to 12.9 per cent). However, this was related primarily to changes in the relative prices of individual commodity groups. The calculation in comparable prices shows an opposite trend, namely a reduction of the share of fuel and other commodities for the same period, and an increase in the share of machinery and equipment.

Soviet imports are characterized by the dominant share of engineering products (34.4 per cent in 1982). Nearly two thirds of the imported equipment comes from the socialist countries of Eastern Europe and one third from the developed market-economy countries. Other goods imported by the USSR include rolled steel and pipes, non-ferrous metals, bauxite, chemical products, phosphate fertilizers, natural rubber, tropical timber and paper. During the period 1960-1981, the relative share of imports of consumer goods and raw materials for the production of consumer goods rose from 23.7 per cent to 33.7 per cent. The Soviet Union imported grain, meat and meat products, sugar, vegetable oil, vegetables, cotton textiles, clothing, footwear, furniture and other consumer items. Imported items constitute nearly 10 per cent of the USSR's retail trade turnover.

## TRADE WITH DEVELOPING COUNTRIES

Yet another feature of trade expansion in the Soviet Union is the emerging importance of the developing countries in its global trade. Soviet policy as stated at the XXVI Congress of the CPU towards the developing countries aims at establishing stable, long-term trade and economic relations with them on the basis of equality and mutual advantage.

The main features of Soviet trade with developing countries are a constant rise in turnover, diversification of the trade pattern and commodity composition, and an ever-growing number of partner countries. In 1971, the Soviet Union maintained direct trade relations with more than 70 developing countries; by 1981 the figure exceeded 100.

In 1970, the turnover was 5.8 billion dollars; in 1982, it was 42.3 billion dollars - a more than sevenfold increase. In 1970, developing countries accounted for 24 per cent of Soviet foreign trade turnover; in 1982, the figure was 26 per cent, or 28 per cent of exports and 23 per cent of imports. At the same time, the USSR's proportion of the aggregate turnover of the developing countries still remains small - about 2 per cent.

The Soviet Union exports machinery, equipment and some other production goods to developing countries. Total machinery and equipment exports to developing countries grew from 0.8 billion roubles in 1970 to 2.6 billion roubles in 1980 - a more than threefold expansion. Along with complete industrial plants, the USSR supplies power equipment, oil-drilling and electrical equipment, metal-cutting machine tools, excavators, road-building machines, tractors, farm machinery, automobiles, ships, navigation equipment, etc. Industrial raw materials and basic products constitute an important part of Soviet exports to developing countries. Deliveries of crude oil and oil products, mineral ores, fertilizers and other items have also increased.

The USSR continues to purchase the traditional export merchandise of developing countries, being a stable market for these goods. It receives from these countries all its imported cocoa beans, coffee, cotton, natural gas and rubber, as well as 75 per cent of its imported skins and hides, over one third of its alumina imports, and one quarter of its imported tin and wool. In 1981, more than half of the Soviet imports from developing countries were foodstuffs (grain, meat, vegetable oil, citrus fruits, bananas, sugar, coffee, cocoa, etc.). Comparing 1981 figures with those of 1970, the volume of imports of these commodities has increased substantially, examples being sugar (4.2 million tons), coffee (41,000 tons), cocoa beans (more than 121,000 tons) and tea (85,000 tons).

Imports of non-traditional items such as machinery, equipment and manufactured consumer goods (clothing, linen, footwear, furniture, pharmaceuticals, etc.), which in 1970 were valued at about 260 million roubles, exceeded 1.9 billion roubles in 1981, accounting for 24.4 per cent of Soviet imports from developing countries.

In its commercial and economic relations with developing countries, the USSR aims to achieve balanced trade, which is reflected in bilateral trade agreements. The deficit of developing countries in their trade with the Soviet Union is covered to a considerable extent by long-term credits, which are granted under intergovernmental agreements on economic and technical co-operation with these countries.

## TARIFFS AND PREFERENCES

The USSR Customs Tariff (1 July 1981) contains a list of goods indicating the duties levied on them when they are exported to the Soviet Union. Goods which correspond to the Soviet Union's Single Commodity Nomenclature of Foreign Trade are classified in the Tariff into nine categories according to their purpose:

1. Machines, equipment and means of transport.

2. Fuels, mineral raw materials, metals.

3. Chemical products, fertilizers, rubber.

4. Construction materials and parts.

5. Raw materials and processed products (other than food) except for those listed above.

6. Live animals.

7. Raw materials for the production of food.

8. Foodstuffs and beverages.

9. Consumer goods.

The USSR Customs Tariff sets import duties which are on the average lower than those in the developed market-economy countries. The Tariff provides for upper and lower rates of duties. Minimal rates are applied to goods which originate in or are imported from countries which apply the Most-Favoured-Nation status to Soviet goods imported by them. It should be emphasized that many goods imported from such countries are duty-free, under the existing tariff. These goods include most types of machines and equipment, raw materials, semi-finished goods and industrial materials, medicines, a number of foodstuffs and some goods serving cultural purposes. Maximum duties, which are also relatively low, are levied on goods which originate in or are imported from countries which do not apply Most-Favoured-Nation status to Soviet goods.

It should be borne in mind that in respect of goods imported from countries which have no trade agreements with the Soviet Union or when such agreements have been violated the Ministry of Foreign Trade can, in consultation with the Ministry of Foreign Affairs and the Ministry of Finances, establish, in accordance with Article 82 of the USSR Customs Tariff, a surcharge on the existing duties or levy duties on duty-free goods.

The customs duties contained in the Tariff are <u>ad valorem</u> and are calculated as a percentage of the c.i.f. port price when goods are carried by sea or franco-frontier of the USSR when they are transported by road, i.e. for the purposes of calculating customs duties the price is composed of the normal wholesale price of the goods in the place of their origin or manufacture plus packaging, insurance, transportation, commissions, export duties and other costs necessary to buy and transport the goods to the Soviet border.

The USSR was the first country that offered duty-free entry to the products of the developing countries. Details of this scheme are given below.

### SCHEME OF THE UNION OF SOVIET SOCIALIST REPUBLICS (USSR)

Date of entry into force: 1 January 1965.

1. Product coverage

Preferences are granted for all agricultural and industrial products. There are no tariff quotas.

2. Depth of tariff cuts

Duty-free entry is granted for all products.

3. Rules of origin

In order to qualify for preferential tariff treatment, goods must have originated in a beneficiary country or must have been imported from such a country.

4. Beneficiaries

The USSR grants preferences to all developing countries of Asia, Africa and Latin America.

The proportion of preferential imports in total Soviet imports from developing countries has increased, as well as the range of such goods and the number of qualifying countries. Textiles represent the largest item among preferential imports from the developing countries. Indeed, yarn, fabrics and clothing account for approximately 26 per cent of all such preferential imports.

### III. FOREIGN TRADE ORGANIZATIONS (FTOS)

The most important trading units are some 60 all-union export-import associations, which are called foreign trade organizations (FTOs). 1/ FTOs are State-owned independent, self-financing legal entities. Their operations are subject to the terms of their statutes, which are approved by the Ministry of Foreign Trade and any other government agency of which they form a part. The export of complete plants and equipment as well as technical assistance services for industrial projects is handled by specialized FTOs operating under the supervision of the State Committee for External Economic Relations.

---

1/  See also chapter II.

FTOs are specialized trading agencies having no manufacturing functions. Each FTO is responsible for a specified range of products or services, so that, as a general rule, a particular product or service is available from a single source only. FTOs are empowered to conclude contracts, enter into other legal arrangements, perform credit and banking operations, issue promissory notes and bills of exchange, sue and be sued, construct, acquire, rent and let property required for their operations both in the USSR and abroad (as well as other real and personal property), establish branch offices, missions and agencies both in the USSR and abroad, and be a partner in various kinds of associations, societies, firms and organizations. The charter of a foreign trade organization lays down the procedure for signing contracts in its name.

Foreign trade organizations vary in structure according to their field of activity, the nature of their goods and the volume of trade. The basic structural unit of a FTO is a specialized firm. A FTO is headed by its director-general, who exercises full power and is responsible for all operations. He is assisted by the board of the organization, made up of foreign trade executives and representatives of the respective ministries, government departments and industrial plants concerned.

The major functions of a FTO are:

(a) Conclusion and fulfilment of transactions with foreign organizations and firms for the export and import of goods;

(b) Placing of orders with the Soviet suppliers of export goods;

(c) Purchase of import goods for the Soviet organizations;

(d) Financial settlements with foreign firms and the Soviet economic organizations connected with the import and export of goods;

(e) Implementation of measures to ensure a high quality of imported and exported goods;

(f) Organization of technical services for the equipment, machinery and instruments sold abroad;

(g) Study of foreign markets and firms with a view to making the best use of market conditions when purchasing or selling goods;

(h) Preparation and submission for review of five-year and annual programmes and their implementation when approved; and

(i) Recommendation of ways of developing new forms of foreign economic relations.

A FTO carries out its transactions on a commission basis.

While a FTO acts as a buying and selling organization on behalf of producing and consuming enterprises and conducts foreign trade, actual purchasing decisions are normally made by the end users - i.e., industrial ministries' enterprises. It must be noted that the internal production and distribution enterprises do not participate as parties to foreign trade contracts.

FTOs normally operate under over-all guidelines laid down by the Ministry of Foreign Trade regarding their entire trading activity. In general, each import contract signed by a FTO requires an import permit from the Ministry of Foreign Trade. Similarly, the FTO concerned must get a licence for any export transactions.

A Soviet enterprise or institute that, in accordance with the foreign trade plan, receives an import permit for the purchase of commodities or equipment abroad, furnishes the relevant FTO with an import requisition showing the commodities to be bought and the specific quantity or value. On the basis of this import order, a FTO approaches a number of foreign firms and, with the participation of the Soviet buyer, selects the best supplier. A FTO must not deviate from the instructions of the import order without the consent of the internal customer. The terms of FTO contracts (e.g., price, quality, delivery date, and payment terms) are usually based on normal commercial considerations.

A FTO pays the domestic customer an indemnity for every day on which the imports are overdue, provided that the delay is not caused by reasons of _force majeure_. If the overdue arrival of part of the import order prevents the use of goods delivered earlier under the same order, the indemnity also takes into account the invoice cost of the earlier imported portion.

In exporting from the USSR, the relevant FTO issues a requisition order to a supplier named in the plan or to an agency authorized in the plan to choose a supplier. The requisition order contains information such as the types of merchandise for delivery, quantity and delivery time. It also includes the number and date of the export permit issued by the Ministry of Foreign Trade. Issuance of the order creates a legal obligation on the part of the enterprise in question to deliver the goods specified, and an obligation on the part of the FTO to accept the goods.

## PROFITABILITY CONCEPT

The FTOs have recently restructured their organization and set up specialized firms within their over-all framework. Each firm specializes in one sector of the FTO sphere of responsibility. FTOs have been encouraged to convert to a self-financing basis.

Permanent export councils have been organized to facilitate more regular consultation between FTOs and industry representatives in the planning and implementation of foreign trade. These councils consist of high-level representatives from production ministries, exporting enterprises and FTOs handling their products. They enable producing enterprises to acquaint FTOs with the possibility of new export products or of additional production of existing export lines.

Another development has been the establishment of specialized associations of _Zagranpostavkas_ (ZPs) to centralize the foreign trade operations of individual production ministries. They are responsible for the punctual fulfilment of export contracts, observance of quality regulations, after-sales service and installation work. In practice, they have usually assumed responsibilities for industrial maintenance and supplies of spare parts for exported equipment.

Most of the two dozen <u>Zagranpostavkas</u> in existence are involved in projects in developing countries, while about a dozen deal with Western firms. They are particularly important in deals involving co-operation and compensation. They are not entitled to conclude foreign trade transactions but advise FTOs on technical specifications and help them draft contracts.

## NEGOTIATIONS WITH FTOS OF THE USSR 1/

A businessman holding negotiations with FTOs of the USSR must keep in mind the following points. This will help to lessen costs, minimize delay and, above all, provide the necessary indicators for the preparation of negotiations.

(a)  Prejudices against dealing with government-owned companies should be discarded. The FTOs of the USSR are government-sponsored bodies but they act in the same way as any commercial organization;

(b)  Since a number of parties are involved in decision-making before a contract is signed, this can result in frequent checking back by the FTOs' representatives with the home authorities;

(c)  Since FTOs are well informed on quality, delivery schedule and prices offered by various suppliers, negotiators from developing countries must also be well prepared on these subjects;

(d)  In a bid to obtain the best offer, the FTOs tend to have parallel negotiations/talks with a number of suppliers simultaneously. It is here that businessmen must assess the market and be prepared to meet this eventuality;

(e)  There are several phases of negotiations: receiving of quotations, competitive offers from FTO to obtain either a price reduction or improvement in terms and conditions of a contract, and the final negotiations;

(f)  Bargaining is part and parcel of the FTO negotiating process. Exporters from developing countries must be aware of this when preparing for negotiations;

(g)  An offer should contain all relevant information - e.g., if detergent powder is being sold, details regarding the quality, price and brand name have to be clearly indicated. In the case of consumer products, a sample accompanying the offer would be of great help;

(h)  It is advisable to keep in continuous contact with one of the leading executives of the FTO with which business relations have been established;

(i)  Importers from developing countries should communicate their requirements to FTOs well in advance, in order to ensure timely deliveries;

---

1/  This procedure is more or less equally valid when dealing with FTOs in other socialist countries of Eastern Europe.

(j)   Since imports and exports are based on the Foreign Trade Plan, it is not always easy to make spot purchases.  It is always advantageous to have long-term contracts for regular deliveries;

(k)   Negotiations with supplying FTOs can be initiated with the trade representatives in the importer's country, followed if necessary by visits to the USSR;

(l)   For complete plant and equipment, interested importers in both the public and private sectors may approach the USSR Economic Counsellor's Office or the FTOs operating under the State Committee for External Economic Relations. Such transactions are usually covered in intergovernmental economic co-operation agreements; and

(m)   When importing machinery and equipment, it would be advisable to ensure supplies of spares and components by incorporating such deliveries in the contract.

One important element of negotiation is the signing of a protocol.  FTOs also sign a protocol with the supplying firm in addition to the contract.  The normal type of protocol signed is given below:

PROTOCOL

The present Protocol is concluded between Messrs ............................ and V/O Soyuzchimexport, Moscow.

The parties agreed hereby on the following:

1.   In accordance with V/O Soyuzchimexport request, Messrs ................ ............................ shall reserve the right and shall commit to sell to V/O Soyuzchimexport, whereby V/O Soyuzchimexport shall intend to buy Denomination of goods:

Quality:

Delivery time:

2.   Price and other terms of delivery will be agreed upon between the parties when contracts are signed, two months prior to the beginning of each year.

3.   Liabilities of the parties in connection with deliveries of the goods (denomination of goods, quantity, delivery) will be effective only in case of signing by the parties of corresponding contracts.

(Signed)   V/O SOYUZCHIMEXPORT     Messrs. X

Careful wording of this protocol will avoid many problems and ensure a smooth flow of business satisfactory to both parties.

## IV.  PRICING IN FOREIGN TRADE

Since the USSR is a planned economy, its internal pricing system is to
a large extent insulated from international prices.  The domestic market
situation may therefore very often lead to considerable misleading conclusions,
due to a marked difference between the international price and the domestic
price.

The USSR accepts world prices as the basis for negotiations in all its
trading relations with non-socialist countries.  Quotation of a f.o.b./c.i.f
price should be carefully prepared.  The USSR normally seeks the FOB price
especially when it has an intergovernmental shipping arrangement.  With
adequate preparation, however, developing countries can quote a suitable
price either f.o.b. or c.i.f. which will be accepted by the Soviet Union if
consistent with its own requirements.  Depending on the market, it is possible
to envisage a stable price for a certain period of time, say six months.

### EXCHANGE RATES AND PRICES

Prices can be quoted in convertible currencies, e.g., US dollars or pounds
sterling, and the impact of possible fluctuations in exchange rates should
be taken into account by seeking cover with the banks in the same way as
is the practice in business transactions with other countries.

In the case of transactions under clearing payments arrangements, the role
of exchange rates should not be neglected.  Business communities will do
well to seek from their respective governments clear guidelines on exchange
rate fluctuations and their implications for business transactions and mutual
trade.  Businessmen could obtain from their governments an explicit written
understanding of various aspects of exchange rates.

## V.  MARKETING TECHNIQUES AND PROMOTIONAL INSTRUMENTS

A developing country firm may adopt various methods of introducing its
export products to the Soviet market:  (a)  if there is a trade or economic
agreement between the company's home country and the USSR, it may try
to get its products included in the agreement;  (b)  it can also promote its
products through the effective use of joint/mixed commissions;  and (c)  it
could sponsor trade delegations from the USSR to acquaint them with its
products.

Developing country companies should, however, make contacts initially
with the FTO responsible for importing and/or exporting the products or
services of interest to them.  FTOs can be contacted in Moscow, or through
their representatives in the Soviet trade representation offices in the
respective developing countries.

As a first step, a developing country firm should send a self-contained
letter containing detailed information about the company and its products
and services to the responsible Soviet FTO.  A copy may also be sent to
the Soviet trade representation office in the company's home country, if
there is one, and to the country's commercial representative in the
Soviet Union.  On receiving a positive response from the FTO, it is advisable
to visit the FTO's office in Moscow.  An invitation from the FTO or other
commercial organizations is mandatory in obtaining the necessary entry visa
for business travel to the USSR.

Subsequently, a foreign firm may use the following techniques to promote its trade with the Soviet Union:

(a)  Arrange symposia in Moscow;

(b)  Distribute technical literature and product literature through the State Public Scientific-Technical Library, Moscow; and

(c)  Advertise in Soviet technical journals through V/O Vneshtorgreklama, 31 Korp. 2 Ul. Kakhovka, Moscow 11346, or one of its representatives abroad.

These techniques will enable a foreign firm to develop contacts with Soviet and users and the relevant industrial ministries and associations, and eventually generate demand for its products and services.  Arranging symposia and exhibitions has proved a successful marketing tool in reaching key decision-makers, including technical experts.  Such events can be arranged through V/O Vneshtorgreklama.  Participation in these symposia and exhibitions can be arranged through the USSR Chamber of Commerce and Industry.

Technical literature and product catalogues sent to the State Public Scientific-Technical Library are circulated to Soviet end users and technical personnel through its network of 82 industrial branches, 15 Republic divisions and about 10,000 information bureaux.  A foreign company is therefore advised to send a sufficient quantity of such material.

## REGULATIONS ON OPENING OFFICES IN MOSCOW

Since State-operated agencies or brokerage enterprises do not exist in the Soviet Union, foreign firms are permitted to set up accredited business offices in Moscow.  A foreign firm interested in opening such an office must submit an application to the Protocol Section of the Ministry of Foreign Trade containing the following information:

(a)  The name of the firm, the date of its formation and its place of residence;

(b)  The nature of its activities, its administrative organ and the persons representing the firm according to its articles of incorporation or articles of agreement;

(c)  The date and place of registration or the articles of incorporation of the firm;

(d)  The authorized capital of the firm;

(e)  The name of the Soviet FTO with which the firm has concluded a transaction, for which purpose an office is required;  and

(f)  The names of the other Soviet FTOs with which the firm has commercial relations.

This information must be supported by documents attached to the application in the form of notarized copies certified in accordance with the established procedure by Soviet consular offices abroad.

The decision whether to allow a foreign company to open an office in Moscow will depend on the volume of the firm's business with the USSR; the length of time for which it has been trading with the USSR; the prospects for continuing business activitiy; and the size and international reputation of the firm. Most cases of accreditation of foreign offices in the USSR are handled by the Ministry of Foreign Trade, the State Committee for Science and Technology or the State Bank of the USSR (GOSBANK). In general, however, the Ministry of Foreign Trade handles accreditation of foreign firms involved in large-scale import and export, and the State Committee for Science and Technology accredits firms handling scientific/industrial/ technological co-operation agreements.

Accreditation is usually valid for one year and renewable annually. An accredited office is required to submit a quarterly report to the Ministry of Foreign Trade concerning its activities, commercial contacts with Soviet organizations, export/import transactions concluded, and the status of their implementation.

An accredited company may employ up to five non-Soviet personnel at its office in Moscow. It may also employ Soviet personnel. All facilities for the normal functioning of a commercial representation office will be provided, including permission to import necessary office machines and equipment, subject to the condition that these items will be exported when no longer required. The name, location and function of an accredited office of a foreign company in Moscow will be listed in the latest issue of suitable business directories.

## TRADE FAIRS AND EXHIBITIONS

Unlike other CMEA member countries, the Soviet Union does not organize international general fairs. Instead, it holds specialized exhibitions. In fact, the USSR is the largest organizer of specialized exhibitions among the socialist countries of Eastern Europe.

The most effective marketing technique for a developing country's exporters is participation in these specialized trade fairs and exhibitions, which enable exhibitors to attract a large number of technical specialists, enterprise managers, engineers and officials who make the ultimate buying decisions. It is also possible to organize independent national exhibitions, as well as smaller exhibitions by individual firms or associations of firms producing similar goods.

Specialized fairs reflect only those industries which are to be expanded under the current or forthcoming Soviet Five-Year Plan. They therefore provide clear indication of what type of equipment, machinery and consumer goods will be demanded in the USSR in the coming years.

To participate in a trade fair or exhibition, exporters from developing countries are advised to get in touch with the USSR Chamber of Commerce and Industry at the following address:

USSR Chamber of Commerce and Industry
6, Ul. Kuibysheva
Moscow 101000, USSR
(Telex: 411126).

To co-ordinate the organization of specialized fairs, a special organization called EXPOCENTRE was set up in 1977 under the control of the USSR Chamber of Commerce and Industry.  All exhibitions in the Soviet Union are sponsored or co-sponsored by this organization in conjunction with the relevant industrial ministry or FTO.  Businessmen may contact this organization for necessary information and application forms for participation in any of the events organized by them.

Most companies participating in specialized fairs hope to maximize their exposure and make contacts to gain greater access to the Soviet market. Soviet officials regard participation in these fairs by foreign firms as an indiciation of serious intention to pursue trade relations with the USSR on a long-term basis.

Soviet FTOs usually do not buy display goods at exhibitions in the USSR. However, there is a good chance of off-the-stand sales.  It is advisable to plan at least six months before the exhibition to sell as many of the displayed items as possible.  This planning calls for consultation with Soviet officials on the choice of exhibits for display.  Off-the-stand sales are valued not so much for the cash proceeds they generate, but for the goodwill they create.

## CHAMBER OF COMMERCE AND INDUSTRY

A non-governmental organization promoting the development of trade, economic, scientific and technical relations with other countries, the USSR Chamber of Commerce and Industry carries out numerous functions.  For newcomers to the Soviet market, the Chamber can be particularly helpful in arranging contacts with officials of FTOs and other organizations.

The Chamber has more than 1,500 members, including FTOs, industrial enterprises and other economic organizations.  It maintains branch offices in large cities throughout the country.  It also has offices in Western Europe and plans to open offices in some of the developing countries. The Chamber's main functions are:

(a)  To develop contacts with foreign business organizations in order to promote trade and economic relations through joint chambers of commerce;

(b)  To invite and act as host to foreign business delegations visiting the USSR and send Soviet delegations abroad;

(c)  To organize Soviet participation in international trade fairs abroad and help arrange foreign exhibitions in the USSR;

(d)  To discharge its role as the patents agent of national organizations that represent the interests of foreign applicants at the State Committee for Inventions and Discoveries;

(e)  To assist Soviet inventors, enterprises and organizations in registering trade-marks and industrial samples abroad, and also foreign citizens and firms in registering their trade-marks and industrial samples in the USSR;

(f) To arrange expert examination and control of the quality and quantity of goods, raw materials and equipment at the request of interested Soviet and foreign organizations, with reciprocal arrangements with foreign quality control organizations to check the goods purchased or sold by the USSR abroad;

(g) To certify force majeure conditions in accordance with the terms of commercial contracts, at the request of interested organizations and persons;

(h) To settle disputes arising in foreign trade and commercial shipping through the Foreign Trade Arbitration Commission, the Maritime Arbitration Commission and the Average Adjusters' Bureau - these being standing bodies functioning under the Chamber;

(i) To handle translation from foreign languages into Russian and vice versa of documents and material concerning foreign trade operations and economic, scientific and technical relations between the USSR and other countries;  and

(j) To issue certificates of origin for Soviet exports.

## VI.  QUALITY CONTROL AND INSPECTION

Soviet foreign trade organizations have standardized the quality definition for their exports by adopting national standards (GOST).  If the GOST norms for any goods do not correspond to the requirements of the world market, a reference is made to the appropriate GOST standard in the contract with a reservation permitting improvement of the quality of the goods in question.

FTOs buy and sell according to generally accepted standards of international trade, particularly commodities - coffee, cocoa, cereals, natural rubber, non-ferrous metals, etc. - whose quality requirements have long been established by commodity exchanges and business associations involved in the production and marketing of these goods.

FTOs also buy and sell goods by sample.  Normally three samples are needed for a deal:  one for the buyer, one for the seller and one for a third party mentioned in the contract, e.g., a chamber of commerce or a company that can check the quality of the goods.  It is usually the buyer who checks whether the goods are equal to sample, with a representative of the seller being present.  In assessing the quality of goods, these organizations do not use such criteria as "good average quality" or "such as it is or will be".

Machinery and equipment are  bought  and sold mostly according to technical terms usually set out by the buyer, and in some cases, by the seller. The quality of some types of machinery and equipment is measured according to international standards.  If there are no national or industrial quality standards for imported goods, contracts with foreign suppliers are concluded only with the agreement of the chief consumer.  When manufactured consumer goods are imported, the importing organization and the supplier establish a guarantee period.  Diagnostic apparatus, drugs and medical equipment for which there are no goverment or industrial standards and which are not on the list of domestically produced products may be imported only by the USSR Ministry of Health, which is entirely responsible for the import of such items.

The quality of Soviet goods intended for export is usually checked by the State Inspection for Quality of Export Goods, which has the status of a Directorate General of the Ministry of Foreign Trade. The State Inspection checks the quality of a large variety of goods, including machines, equipment, instruments, forestry goods, etc. For other goods, certificates of quality are issued by other special State inspection bodies, e.g., the State Grain Inspection, the Inspection for Quality of Textile Raw Materials, the State Inspection for Quality of Seeds, etc., working under the corresponding ministries and departments.

Most export contracts signed by Soviet foreign trade corporations contain a clause stating the buyer's agreement to regard the certificates issued by Soviet inspection agencies as final and indisputable.

## VII. BANKING IN THE USSR

### THE STATE BANK OF THE USSR (GOSBANK)

The State Bank of the USSR (GOSBANK), which is the Central Bank of the USSR, serves as the financial apparatus of the Government and is responsible directly to the Council of Ministers. It participates in the formulation of financial plans and controls the financial implementation of the economic plan. Its functions include issuing and clearing, supplying credit to USSR enterprises and keeping their accounts, and controlling distributed funds. GOSBANK holds the USSR's gold and a part of the foreign exchange reserves, establishes exchange rates, and plans and regulates currency circulation. The rouble is used only for domestic transactions, its export or import being prohibited by law.

GOSBANK also extends accreditation to the representative offices of foreign banks, whose main activities concern the protection and extension of inter bank relations established with the Bank for Foreign Trade of the USSR (Vneshtorgbank) and CMEA banks - IBEC and IIB.

### THE BANK FOR FOREIGN TRADE OF THE USSR (VNESHTORGBANK)

Vneshtorgbank is the international arm of the Soviet banking system. One of the world's largest banks, with total assets of 40.5 billion roubles as of 1 January 1981, Vneshtorgbank is a joint stock company in which GOSBANK and several other Soviet organizations are shareholders. Although operationally independent, it is subject to general policy supervision by GOSBANK.

In financing Soviet foreign trade, Vneshtorgbank performs all functions normally carried out by commercial banks elsewhere. It opens accounts in Soviet and foreign currencies and accepts deposits from Soviet and foreign juridical persons, individuals and international organizations. It finances Soviet foreign trade by granting credits and settles accounts involved in export and import trade, as well as rendering other related services such as establishing and making payments under letters of credit, and settling accounts on non-commercial payments abroad. It also guarantees financial liabilities to Soviet and foreign juridical persons, handles operations with promissory notes and bills of exchange and buys and sells foreign currency, bullion and precious metals, etc.

In performing its operations, the Vneshtorgbank uses conventional methods and adheres to the Customs and Practices for Documentary Credits (1974) of the International Chamber of Commerce. The Bank has correspondent relationships with over 1,700 banks in more than 110 countries, including almost all large Western banks, which readily confirm letters of credit issued by Vneshtorgbank. In addition to financing foreign trade, Vneshtorgbank handles the settlement of clearing balances under the USSR's bilateral payment arrangements.

## METHODS AND TERMS OF PAYMENT

All the usual terms of payment, ranging from cash down payment to long-term credit for 8-10 years, are used in the USSR. For urgently needed imports, Soviet FTOs may be willing to pay cash, even if considerable amounts are involved. For other imports, FTOs may insist on credit terms, varying from 90 to 180 days.

Cash transactions are handled on a cash against documents (c.a.d.) basis. The exporter's bank send the documents to Vneshtorgbank in Moscow, which normally pays within 8-10 days after receiving them. For imports, FTOs may establish letters of credit with Vneshtorgbank, giving the usual conditions of shipment. When buying plant and machinery, FTOs generally ask for deferred payment terms, which may extend up to 10 years. Similarly, when exporting plant and machinery, FTOs also offer deferred payment credit terms.

## VIII. MARKETING LOGISTICS

### SHIPPING

The Soviet Union has signed several bilateral and other maritime agreements which provide for port access and sharing of cargo between the signatory countries.

There are two organizations - V/O Sovfracht and V/O Sovinflot - responsible for maritime transportation. V/O Sovfracht performs brokerage functions, including chartering of Soviet ships for carriage of cargoes of foreign charterers, and chartering of foreign dry cargo tramp and tanker tonnage for carriage of cargoes of Soviet FTOs. It also serves as a broker in chartering agreements between foreign shipowners and charterers.

As a general agent of Soviet shipping companies, V/O Sovinflot organizes agency services, stevedore bunkering and other services for Soviet ships in foreign ports, including the supply of fuel and lubricants. In the field of liner shipping, V/O Sovinflot co-ordinates the activities of Soviet shipping companies within the framework of Liner Conferences, pools and similar organizations; secures cargoes for Soviet lines on a long-term basis through agents and other firms; organizes the carriage, agency servicing and forwarding of container cargoes; and also rents containers and container equipment.

## TRANSPORTATION

SOYUZVNESHTRANS is another organization dealing with transportation in the USSR. It handles transportation and forwarding operations connected with Soviet foreign trade. It organizes transportation of goods by sea, rail, river, motorway and air, and is also responsible for organizing transportation of transit goods through Soviet territory from European countries to countries of the Near, Middle and Far East and vice versa by all methods. It also handles transportation and forwarding of exhibition goods in ports and at border stations.

## AIR

Aeroflot, the Soviet airline, offers a regular air cargo service to many destinations in the world. A number of foreign airlines also offer regular air cargo services to locations in the USSR.

## MAJOR PORTS

The chief ports are Odessa, Nikolaev, Novorossisk, Batum, Leningrad, Murmansk, Nakhodka, Vladivostok and the new port of Vostochny, as well as the Latvian ports of Riga and Liyepaya.

## INSURANCE

Foreign trade insurance administration in the USSR is handled by INGOSSTRAKH, a joint stock company, which undertakes all classes of property and personal insurance and reinsurance both on the territory of the USSR and abroad, including transport insurance for cargo ships, insurance of property against fire and natural calamity, insurance of motor vehicles, and civil liability and accident insurance.

INGOSSTRAKH performs its operations either directly or through its wide network of representatives in the USSR and abroad: it has three wholly owned subsidiaries in London, Hamburg and Vienna. It undertakes to settle claims in any currency.

## IX.  CONTRACTS AND DOCUMENTATION

## CONTRACTS

While intra-CMEA trade is governed by the "General Terms of CMEA Deliveries", in trading with non-socialist countries, Soviet FTOs use extensively the internationally accepted general contract terms. Such contracts specify standard terms such as force majeure, arbitration, sanctions, guarantees, inspection tests, acceptance of goods, transportation conditions etc.

## ARBITRATION

FTOs try to settle all disputes directly with the trading partner whenever possible, and many have never resorted to official arbitration. They do not normally insist on arbitration in Moscow and the most common provision in contracts allows for arbitration in a mutually acceptable third country.

If arbitration in Moscow is agreed upon, the disputes are handled by the Foreign Trade Arbitration Commission of the USSR Chamber of Commerce and Industry (in the case of exports and imports) or by the Chamber's Maritime Arbitration Commission in the case of maritime disputes.

Each party chooses one arbitrator from the panel of 15 Soviet citizens (25 in the case of the Maritime Arbitration Commission). The two arbitrators then choose a third as the chairman. Each arbitrator has an equal vote. Award is by a majority vote. The awards are final and binding upon both parties. An award that is not carried out by the party within the time indicated is enforced under the civil court procedure of the USSR. If enforcement is sought outside the USSR, the laws of the respective country are applicable.

## DOCUMENTATION

The documentary requirements for each shipment to the USSR, irrespective of value or mode of transport, will be specified in the covering contract, including the number of copies of each document, its content and the language in which it is to be written. The documents usually required are:

(a) Commercial invoice. Data usually required under the terms of a contract are the country of origin, details of packing materials, marking on and number of packages, weights (net, gross and tare), quality and description of goods, unit prices and total shipment value, selling price and place of final despatch. Besides the contract number, the import licence number must appear on the invoice;

(b) Certificate of origin. Required only when requested by the importer. When a chamber of commerce certification must be obtained, an additional notarized copy is required for the chamber's files;

(c) Bill of lading. No special requirements. The import licence number (as well as the contract number) must be shown;

(d) Packing list. Besides a complete and explicit summary of the shipment, this must also contain contract and import licence numbers;

(e) Insurance certificate. The terms of the contract determine whether the seller or buyer obtains insurance; and

(f) Import licence. All goods must be covered by an import licence or permit.

## X. TRANSFER OF TECHNOLOGY

The State determines the development of its foreign economic, scientific and technological co-operation. The transfer of technology to developing countries from the USSR takes place primarily through intergovernmental agreements. These agreements, which provide a framework for direct contacts at the operative level, fall into the following categories:

(a) Agreements concerning trade and payments. In this case, transfer of technology is treated as any other sale or purchase of goods or services;

(b)   Agreements on scientific and technical co-operation;   and

(c)   Agreements on economic co-operation, covering sale of complete plants, when technology is partly embodied in the machinery and equipment, and partly transferred separately in the study, design and production processes and in technical assistance connected with making the plant operational and training personnel.

Some 19 agreements have been signed between the USSR and developing countries for technology transfer.

Typical features of agreements for scientific and technological co-operation are:  exchange of scientific and technical delegations and personnel or other specialists;  exchange of scientific and technical documentation and information;  supply of studies and engineering designs; organization of scientific and technical conferences, seminars and exhibitions; joint work on scientific, technical and technological problems, with the possibility of introducing the results achieved into industrial production, agriculture and other areas of the economy;  practical and theoretical training of personnel, etc.

A rapidly growing method of technology transfer to developing countries in which the USSR participates is through tripartite industrial co-operation, joining together partners from socialist countries, developed market-economy countries and developing countries.

Technology is purchased by the USSR on the basis of the guidelines issued by the Gosplan.  The applicant for purchase of technology must defend his case for turning to outside markets and establish the advantages over the USSR's indigenous technology resources.  The terms and conditions for the sale and purchase of technology, including licensing arrangements and co-production agreements, are negotiable.

CHAPTER VI

TRADING WITH BULGARIA

1. ECONOMY

The People's Republic of Bulgaria, with a territory of 110,000 sq. kilometres, is situated in South-East Europe, bounded to the north by Romania and to the east by the Black Sea. Turkey and Greece lie to the south and Yugoslavia to the west. It has a population of about 8.9 million.

CHARACTERISTIC FEATURES OF THE BULGARIAN ECONOMY

The Bulgarian economy is characterized by public ownership of the means of production. Industry is divided into 81 State economic corporations. Agriculture is organized into 282 agro-industrial complexes - large production units with a high degree of concentration (average area 14,000 hectares) and specialization. Economic activity, including foreign trade, is planned on the basis of annual, five-year and long-term national economic plans. Bulgaria has relatively few ore and mineral resources, these consisting mainly of lignite, brown coal, copper and lead-zinc ores, marble and quartz-sand.

STRUCTURE OF THE ECONOMY

During the last decade (1970-1981), the annual growth rates of basic indicators characterizing Bulgaria's economic development were the following: gross domestic product (GDP) increased on average by 6.7 per cent, national income by 6.8 per cent, industrial production by 7.2 per cent, agricultural production by 2.3 per cent, capital investment by 6.7 per cent, retail trade by 5.7 per cent and real income per capita by 4.2 per cent.

The share of agriculture in the national income has declined from 23 per cent in 1970 to 16 per cent in 1981 (1939 = 83 per cent), whereas the share of industry increased to 49 per cent in 1981 (1939 = 15 per cent). Major industries are energy, metallurgy, machine building, electrical engineering and chemicals. The growth of the metallurgy industry has been spectacular: production of steel and pig iron has increased substantially and there is also a well developed non-ferrous metal industry. Machine building is an important activity, supplying 25 per cent of total industrial output. Priority has been accorded to electrical power equipment such as electrical motors, transformers, generators, etc. Hoisting and handling equipment, electronics and electrical engineering, may be classified as the leading sectors of the machine building industry. Bulgaria is the world's largest per capita producer and one of the biggest exporters of electric forklift trucks and hoists. Next come the food/beverages industry, followed by chemicals and pharmaceuticals and textiles. Bulgaria ranks first in world per capita output of calcinated soda, blue vitriol and cigarettes and is among the leading producers of woollen, cotton and synthetic yarns, nitrogen fertilizers, sulphuric acid, tomatoes and wheat.

The national Five-Year Plan currently in force (1981-1985) aims at an annual economic growth of 3.7 per cent. Capital investment is targeted to increase each year, on average, by 0.9 per cent, industrial production by 5.1 per cent, agricultural production by 3.4 per cent and foreign trade by 6.9 per cent. Major industries to be accorded high priority include power generation, ferrous and non-ferrous metallurgy, heavy investment machinery, electronics, industrial robots and chemicals.

## II.  FOREIGN TRADE

Bulgaria has a limited internal market and also suffers from a certain scarcity of natural resources.  It therefore depends on foreign trade for developing its economy.  Expansion of production far in excess of domestic demand means that a large number of products are designed for export.  One significant feature is that the rate of growth in foreign trade is higher than the rate of growth in national income and industrial production.  Thus, for the period 1970-1982, exports grew annually by 14.9 per cent and imports by 14.0 per cent.

In absolute terms, exports went up from foreign exchange 2,004 million dollars in 1970 to 11,440 million dollars in 1982.  Similarly, imports have grown from 1,831 million dollars in 1970 to 11,540 million dollars in 1982.  Foreign trade accounts for 85 per cent of the country's national income.

### COMPOSITION OF TRADE

Exports consist mainly of manufactured items.  The share of machines and equipment in total exports has risen from 29.0 per cent in 1970 to 45.8 per cent in 1981.

Within the framework of the CMEA, Bulgaria has been entrusted with specialization in the production of a number of relatively new basic export items.  At the same time, due to scarce local natural resources, industrial demand is likely to remain the leading factor for the stable increase in imports of industrial raw materials.

There has been a sharp decline in exports of agricultural products as a result of the diminishing importance of agriculture, on the one hand, and increased consumption at home, on the other.  The share of raw materials and food products in exports fell from 51.5 per cent in 1970 to 37.5 per cent in 1981.

Bulgaria imports a considerable amount of machinery and equipment, raw materials and fuels.  These commodity groups constituted 88.1 per cent of total imports in 1981.

### DIRECTION OF TRADE

Table 3 shows the geographical distribution of Bulgaria's foreign trade.

The most important feature of the geographical distribution of Bulgarian trade in the post-war period has been the involvement of CMEA member countries. In 1982, 75.6 per cent of Bulgarian exports were directed to socialist countries of Eastern Europe, and these countries supplied 74.3 per cent of Bulgarian imports.  Developed market-economy countries accounted for 12.2 per cent of exports and 16.9 per cent of imports in 1982.

Table 3

Foreign trade of the People's Republic of Bulgaria: 1970 and 1982
(Value in millions of dollars f.o.b.)

| Geographical distribution | Exports | | Imports | |
|---|---|---|---|---|
| | 1970 | 1982 | 1970 | 1982 |
| Total trade | 2 004 | 11 440 | 1 831 | 11 540 |
| of which: | | | | |
| Developing countries | 200 | 2 246 | 142 | 993 |
| Per cent of total | 10.0 | 19.6 | 7.8 | 8.6 |
| Developed market-economy countries | 289 | 1 398 | 355 | 1 945 |
| Per cent of total | 14.4 | 12.2 | 19.4 | 16.9 |
| Socialist countries of Eastern Europe | 1 514 | 7 769 | 1 333 | 8 576 |
| Per cent of total | 75.6 | 68.0 | 72.8 | 74.3 |

Source: UNCTAD, "Trends and policies in trade and eocnomic co-operation among countries having different economic and social systems"; Statistical annex (TD/B/1003/Add.1).

TRADE WITH DEVELOPING COUNTRIES

Bulgaria maintains active trade and economic relations with more than 70 developing countries in Africa, Asia and Latin America. The share of developing countries in Bulgarian exports increased from 10.0 per cent in 1970 to 19.6 per cent in 1982; but their share in imports was only 8.6 per cent in 1982, having increased from 7.8 per cent in 1970. In absolute terms, Bulgarian exports to developing countries have increased from 200 million dollars in 1970 to 2,246 million dollars in 1982. Imports have grown from 142 million dollars in 1970 to 993 million dollars in 1982.

The major items exported to developing countries are: complete plants (food, textiles, tobacco), metal-cutting machines, power equipment, electric forklift trucks, tractors, transport and construction equipment, chemicals and pharmaceutical products and various consumer goods and foodstuffs.

Bulgaria's imports from developing countries include traditional items such as tea, coffee, cocoa, spices, soya beans, industrial raw materials and fuels - iron ore, raw phosphate, crude oil, rubber and jute - and, more recently, industrial products such as electrical equipment, cable and telex machinery, fertilizers, tyres, construction equipment, shoes and leather goods, textiles, pharmaceutical products, clothing, knitwear and handicrafts.

Bulgaria's policy towards countries with different economic and social systems, and in particular to developing countries, is to expand foreign trade on a mutually advantageous and balanced basis. As a result, its trade balance with many developing countries is in equilibrium. At the same time, some developing countries such as Brazil, Tunisia and Peru maintain surpluses. Other developing countries have deficits in their trade with Bulgaria, which are mainly due to imports of capital equipment on the basis of long-term credits, the repayment of which is deferred for long periods. Major trade partners among the developing countries are the Arab States (including North Africa) and the Islamic Republic of Iran, followed by the Asian, African and Latin American countries.

The Bulgarian Government encourages foreign trade orgnaizations to increase their imports of various commodities and other goods from the developing countries directly, instead of through intermediary trading companies in Western Europe. Anxious to maintain balanced trade relations with the developing countries, Bulgaria directs its overseas purchases to those countries with which it has an export surplus. Special efforts are also made to increase the purchase of semi-manufactured and manufactured goods from the developing countries.

Bulgaria's foreign trade plans do not include targets concerning or influencing the choice of trading partners within a given type of currency. The decision in this respect is taken by the economic organization on purely commercial considerations, proceeding from the world market situation and the exchange rates of the currency involved, so that the most competitive offer may be selected. The foreign trade plan does not create import demand by itself, nor does it constitute an import restriction, since it is a reflection of the requirements of the country's national economy against the background of the payments resources available.

Along with expansion of foreign trade, various forms of mutual economic co-operation have developed in recent years. Bulgaria has concluded diversified industrial, technical, scientific and cultural co-operation agreements with more than 75 developing countries in Asia, Africa and Latin America. On this basis, Bulgarian specialized organizations have undertaken construction projects in developing countries in industry (machine building, electronics and electrical engineering, pharmaceuticals, construction, food, tobacco and beverages, etc.), agriculture (pilot farms, agro-industrial complexes, greenhouses for vegetables and flowers, etc.) and infrastructure (river and sea ports, airports, highways, etc.).

The further extension of economic co-operation between Bulgaria and developing countries is expected to improve prospects for stable and balanced trade. The developing countries, for their part, could utilize the potential of the Bulgarian market by improving the quality and terms of delivery and establishin direct contacts with Bulgarian trading enterprises.

## FOREIGN TRADE INSTRUMENTS

Bulgaria emphasizes the importance of intergovernmental agreements for promoting trade. An important point here is the country's steady shift away from clearing payments arrangements to payments in convertible currencies. In fact, Bulgaria aims to multilateralize all its payments arrangements. In consequence, the vast majority of payments (more than 95 per cent) in its trade relations with the developing countries are made in convertible currencies. Nevertheless, Bulgaria is flexible in this respect and usually agrees to retain specific bilateral payments arrangements when this is considered by both partners to be mutually advantageous.

## TARIFF PREFERENCES FOR DEVELOPING COUNTRIES

Bulgaria's import tariff structure is in conformity with the Brussels Tariff Nomenclature. It has four columns - column one gives preferential rates for imports from the least developed countries; column two contains rates for the other developing countries; column three contains rates for imports from countries that grant MFN treatment to Bulgaria, and column four contains rates for imports from countries that do not grant MFN treatment to Bulgaria. The tariffs are applied ad valorem. The dutiable value is determined on the basis of the purchase price of the imported goods and all insurance and transport costs up to the Bulgarian border.

Details of Bulgaria's GSP scheme for developing countries, which came into force on 1 April 1972 and was improved in 1981, are given below.

### BENEFICIARIES

In general, Bulgaria grants preferences to all developing countries. However, the Government reserves the right not to grant preferences to those countries whose per capita national income is higher than that of Bulgaria or to those whose trade policy discriminates against Bulgaria.

### PRODUCT COVERAGE

Preferences are granted for all agricultural and industrial products.

There are no tariff quotas and other restrictive provisions.

### DEPTH AND SCOPE OF TARIFF CUTS

Bulgaria grants a zero rate of duty to the least developed countries. The tariff reduction for items in chapters 1-24 of the scheme is 50 per cent, and for chapters 25-29 it is 20-50 per cent of the MFN rates. The scheme has been altered regarding commodity composition and now covers the entire Bulgarian customs tariffs. As a result, the share of industrial goods imported from developing countries has increased significantly.

### RULES OF ORIGIN

In order to qualify for preferential tariff treatment, goods eligible for preferences must comply with specified origin criteria. Goods are considered to have originated in a beneficiary country if they are entirely produced in that country or if the unknown origin does not exceed 50 per cent of their cost. In this connection, Bulgaria regards all beneficiary countries as one area for the purposes of defining origin (cumulative origin). Direct consignment is required. The goods for which preferential tariff treatment is claimed must be accompanied by a certificate of origin (Form A of the generalized system of preferences) with an exception for imports up to $5,000 in value.

### III. ROLE AND FUNCTIONS OF FOREIGN TRADE ORGANIZATIONS (FTOS)

Bulgarian FTOs are special State organizations granted commercial and financial autonomy in all areas. The authorization to engage in foreign trade activities and the scope of these activities are determined by the Council of Ministers, FTOs are economically independent juridical bodies and bear no responsibility for liabilities of the State, and <u>vice versa</u>.

The principal functions of these organizations are: to inform the economic (producer) organizations of conditions on the international markets; to carry out all activities related to the export of goods produced in the country and to the import of required goods; to participate in the preparation, conclusion and implementation of contracts and agreements on economic co-operation and on specialization and co-operation in production; to assist in creating links between production at home and the international markets, as well as in the introduction of new products and in the expansion of export output; to participate in international fairs and exhibitions; and to organize and conduct advertising abroad.

FTOs may participate in: foreign-based firms, independently or on a partnership basis; international economic organizations of the CMEA member countries; the joint construction and exploitation of projects at home and abroad with foreign organizations and firms; joint purchases and utilization of licences and engineering with foreign firms; and the conclusion of contracts for servicing machines and equipment.

The improved mechanism of planned national economic management envisages a further evolution of financially self-supporting foreign trade enterprises with a view to achieving optimal growth and diversification of exports and imports and increasing their efficiency. The long-term trend of strengthening economic incentives continues to play an increasingly active role in improving the organizational framework of foreign trade, while direct organizational and economic links between internal production units and FTOs are constantly encouraged.

Relations between economic organizations and FTOs are based on contracts. The manufacturers of goods for export freely negotiate the kinds and quantities of goods with FTOs, bearing in mind the mandatory fulfilment of the State plan indicator for the receipt of foreign exchange. FTOs handle exports and imports on a commission basis, in their own name, but on behalf of the economic organization which produces the goods. They are also entitled to make export and import deals on their own account. Should a specialized FTO fail to conclude a contract for a certain kind of commodity in good time, or to secure the expected results, the economic (producer) organization has the right to conclude a contract with another FTO. When deals are made on commission, the FTO must agree on prices and conditions with the economic organization that has produced, or is to purchase, the respective commodity. It is the FTO that is a party to foreign trade contracts; it finances the activity with its own funds and with bank loans.

FTOs are, in fact, economic organizations for import, export and services, with a marked specialization in commodities. Depending on the form of ownership, they may belong to the State or to a co-operative; depending on the level of management, they may be a corporation/association/enterprise, company, foreign trade directorate or office.

FTOs are specialized buying and selling organizations with a high degree of commercial and financial autonomy in all their activities. They are well informed regarding sources of supply. Primarily, they operate through their commercial representatives in developing countries, but also contact sellers/buyers participating in exhibitions and trade fairs and respond to letters addressed to them. The commercial representatives may conclude transactions and perform other legal actions on behalf of the account of the Bulgarian FTO only when they are specifically authorized to do so.

Bulgarian FTOs trade on the basis of world prices. It is important that the seller should specify the time period for which the price remains valid. This would guard against increased costs in the event of a long time lag between the final price quotations and the signing of the contract, c.i.f. or f.o.b. quotations are acceptable. Prices can be quoted in US dollars or other convertible currencies.

Balancing of imports and exports is a very important factor, although it may not always apply. In order to achieve this balance, Bulgarian FTOs have recourse to various forms of transactions, in particular compensation agreements. To facilitate this form of trade, the FTOs exercise considerable flexibility in their commercial transactions. Every FTO is authorized to participate in such trade under the supervision of the industrial ministry to which it is responsible. The Ministry of Foreign Trade issues the necessary import and export licences.

## JOINT VENTURES

The development of co-operation in production and other spheres has led to joint ventures which, in recent years, have become a promising form of economic co-operation. At present more than 40 joint firms work in various countries, including India, the Islamic Republic of Iran, Iraq, the Lebanon and Nigeria. In joint-stock ventures, Bulgaria's share usually amounts to less than 50 per cent, which enables the developing countries to exercise full control of their activities. Bulgaria's participation usually takes the form of providing machinery and equipment, technical documentation and materials necessary for the operation of the joint venture, as well as technical assistance through provision of experts and technology. Areas of economic co-operation in which Bulgaria has specialized are: agro-industrial complexes, mining and processing of non-ferrous metals, timber-based industries, pharmaceutical products and mechanical and electrical engineering.

The Government has issued a Special Decree (No. 535) stipulating the terms and conditions of joint ventures covering various fields of economic co-operation in Bulgaria and other countries.

## IV. MARKETING AND TRADE PROMOTION

### AGENCY NETWORK

As early as 1955, a bureau for representation of foreign firms was set up in the Bulgarian Chamber of Commerce, becoming an independent organization under a decree of December 1975. Commercial representation of foreign firms in Bulgaria is subject to the requirements of the State foreign trade monopoly. In practice this means that foreign firms may ask one of the specialized offices of the Interpred association to act as their agent and the latter requests permission from the Ministry of Foreign Trade.

Eleven independent offices under Interpred guidance now represent more than 800 foreign firms on the basis of an agency contract between the foreign company and a particular bureau. These offices work for a retainer fee, which varies with the size of the account and range of services to be rendered. Any contract between a foreign firm and Interpred has to be validated by the Ministry of Foreign Trade. Interpred is well known for keeping commercial secrets.

A foreign firm that has signed up an Interpred office to represent it in Bulgaria can, through the agency, rent office space and hire local staff. The firm can temporarily import office equipment and vehicles for its use duty-free. However, at the termination of the agency agreement, these items must be re-exported. Interpred offices can provide the following services:

(a) Arrange contacts with Bulgarian FTOs;

(b) Help in the negotiation of sales contracts;

(c) Provide secretariat assistance;

(d) Arrange product testing;

(e) Undertake maintenance of machinery;

(f) Store spare parts;

(g) Hold symposia and conferences;

(h) Arrange participation in the Plovdiv Fair; and

(i) Arrange consultations with competent ministries.

The decree of 1975 also permits foreign firms with long-established business contacts in Bulgaria and involved in reciprocal purchase agreements with Bulgarian enterprises to establish their own temporary representation offices in Bulgaria. A company availing itself of this facility also pays a commission to its Interpred representative on every sale in Bulgaria. Office space and local staff have to be arranged through Interpred.

For a foreign firm to open its own representation office, Interpred has to apply for a permit to the Ministry of Foreign Trade. The permit is usually granted for two years. Foreign firms may employ their own personnel up to the number of Bulgarian staff employed at the office. All appointments with the Government and with foreign trade enterprises have to be arranged through the Protocol Division of the Interpred association.

Interpred offices are organized by territory and language. They are autonomous juridical persons, independent of each other, but directed and co-ordinated by the Interpred association. The address of the association is: Stamboliiski Boul. 2, Sofia, Bulgaria (Telex: 022 284 and 022 794/Cables: INTERPRED/Telephone: 87-45-21 and 87-31-91/96).

Operating through a representation agency can be particularly helpful for a developing country firm entering Bulgaria for the first time, as the agent has first-hand knowledge of current business practices and close contacts with trading/producing organizations.

## BULGARIAN CHAMBER OF COMMERCE AND INDUSTRY

The Chamber of Commerce and Industry is a public organization.  Membership includes the economic ministries and State committees, economic organizations, corporations and economic combines, foreign and home trade organizations, industrial enterprises and agro-industrial complexes, banks, and transport, tourist and other enterprises.  It operates on an independent budget.  Its activities are aimed at promoting trade and economic co-operation with foreign currencies on the basis of mutual interest and benefit, and its functions are as follows:

(a)  To study the economy at home and abroad and to assist in the establishment, expansion and intensification of economic ties and co-operation between Bulgarian economic organizations and foreign firms;

(b)  To intensify Bulgarian participation in socialist economic integration with the CMEA member countries;

(c)  To promote the expansion of industrial co-operation with the developing and developed market-economy countries;

(d)  To assist industry, construction, transport, farming and other branches of the national economy in achieving technological progress and in expanding the variety and improving the quality of consumer goods;

(e)  To organize Bulgarian participation in world and national exhibitions, in international fairs and similar undertakings, and to assist the participation of Bulgarian economic organizations;

(f)  To provide arbitration in disputes between Bulgarian and foreign firms.

The international activities of the Chamber have been intensified in recent years.  A number of agreements have been signed with similar institutions abroad, including 26 organizations in developing countries, for bilateral co-operation involving exchange of business delegations.  The Chamber has also developed close ties with relevant international non-governmental economic organizations, especially with the International Chamber of Commerce in Paris.

The Bulgarian Chamber undertakes various activities to expand business contacts between domestic enterprises and foreign companies.  It organizes the International Plovdiv Fair and also handles Bulgaria's participation in more than 30 international trade fairs abroad.

## TRADE FAIRS AND EXHIBITIONS

The most important single shop window for foreign trade with Bulgaria is the International Plovdiv Fair, which celebrated its 90th anniversary in 1982.  It is held twice a year - in May for consumer goods and in September for technical goods - on an exhibition space of 170,000 sq. metres and with the participation of more than 47 countries, including about 20 developing countries. Representatives of most of the production ministries, corporations, factories, and foreign trade enterprises visit the Fair, thus providing a useful way for business circles in developing countries to make commercial impact and establish contact with prospectiv_ buying and selling organizations.

## V. QUALITY CONTROL AND INSPECTION

Bulgarian FTOs have standardized quality definition for exports by adopting national standards (BDS). If the norms for any goods do not correspond to the requirements of the world market, reference is made to the appropriate BDS standard in the contract, with a reservation allowing for improvement in the quality of the goods in question. If there are no national or industrial quality standards for imported goods, contracts with foreign suppliers are concluded only with the agreement of the chief consumer.

The following institutions are entrusted with the task of quality control and inspection:

1. Bulgarkontrola, 42 Parchevitch St., Sofia, is a specialized institution which may be requested to control the quality of goods as a third party according to a legal agreement. Bulgarkontrola has offices in all major industrial, trade and transportation centres in the country and has at its disposal laboratories for quality control of chemicals and textiles.

2. The Inspectorate for the Quality of Export Goods, 16 Lenin Sq., Sofia, functions as an independent, specialized subdivision of the Ministry of Foreign Trade.

3. The Sanitary-Epidemiological Board, 5 Lenin Sq., Sofia, operating under the Ministry of Health, is a specialized institution for checking standards of hygiene and other requirements for the manufacture, processing, transportation, storage and sale of foodstuffs, as well as products that might present health hazards for consumers.

4. The Inspectorate for Veterinary Control and Quarantine, 1 Rabotnicheska Klasa St., Sofia, operating under the Ministry of Agriculture and Food Industry, controls through border stations the export, import and transit of live animals, foodstuffs and technical raw materials, as well as fodder and materials that may carry infection.

5. The Chief Inspectorate for Approval and Control of Seeds, 6 Dragon Cankov Blvd., Sofia, is an independent department under the Ministry of Agriculture and Food Industry. It is entirely responsible for production, approval, purchase, storage, transportation, export, import, sowing and planting of seeds, in order to meet national requirements (and provide reserves for export) of top quality pure seeds and planting materials.

6. The Board of Patents and Trademarks, at the Bulgarian Chamber of Commerce and Industry is responsible for all matters related to the protection of industrial property. The Board is the sole representative of foreign physical and juridical bodies wishing to obtain patents for their inventions or to register trade markets in Bulgaria.

## VI. BANKING SYSTEM

Bulgaria has two main banks - the Bulgarian National Bank and the Bulgarian Foreign Trade Bank. There is also a State Savings Fund where individuals can deposit their savings and obtain loans.

The Bulgarian National Bank performs the functions of a bank of issue and payments and provides the country's economic organizations, ministries and departments with all kinds of credits in national currency. Since all State enterprises and institutions, except foreign trade establishments, deposit funds with it and obtain credits from it, the Bulgarian National Bank exercises financial control over the country's economic activities.

The Bulgarian Foreign Trade Bank has been assigned the functions of providing credit for the activities of the country's FTOs and of handling all payments operations abroad. The Bank maintains correspondent relationships with banking institutions throughout the world. It undertakes the sale and purchase of foreign currency and provides credits, in the national and in foreign currencies, for the activities of foreign trade enterprises. It also handles all payments to and from member countries of CMEA and co-operates very closely with the International Bank for Economic Co-operation, Moscow, for the settlement of transactions in transferable countries.

## METHODS AND TERMS OF PAYMENT

All the usual terms of payment, ranging from cash payment to long-term credit for 8-10 years, are in use. For urgently needed imports, Bulgarian FTOs may be willing to pay cash, even if considerable amounts are involved. For other imports, FTOs may insist on credit terms, varying from 90 to 180 days.

Cash transactions are handled on a cash against documents (c.a.d.) basis. The exporter's bank sends the documents to the Bulgarian Foreign Trade Bank in Sofia, which normally pays after receiving them. For imports, FTOs may establish letters of credit with the Foreign Trade Bank, giving the usual conditions of shipment. When buying plant and machinery, FTOs generally ask for deferred payment terms, which may extend up to 10 years. Similarly, when exporting plant and machinery, FTOs also offer deferred payment credit terms.

## VII. MARKETING LOGISTICS

### SHIPPING

The National Transport Complex, which operates under the guidance of the Ministry of Transport, is responsible for conducting the unified State policy in the field of transport.

The Water Transport State economic association is responsible for the transport of cargoes by sea and river. It is engaged in the repair of vessels and relevant equipment, the handling and shipment of cargoes, the building and maintenance of harbours and harbour installations, piloting and towing of ships, and connected research work. Three enterprises that belong to this economic association are: the Bulgarian Merchant Fleet, the Bulgarian Tanker Fleet and the Bulgarian River Fleet. The Bulgarian Merchant Fleet transports dry cargoes by sea, using liner and tramp ships. The Bulgarian Tanker Fleet handles the transport of oil products, vegetable oil, wine, etc., to and from all parts of the world. The Bulgarian River Fleet handles the transport by river of dry and liquid cargo. The major ports on the Danube are Ruse, Lom, Vidin, Somovit and Svishtov. The Inflot State Forwarding Enterprise offers agency services.

## TRANSPORTATION

Shippers may sign contracts for transport only with the representatives of the Transpred General Board. Transpred plans and co-ordinates all transport services and shipment of goods, whether by container, rail, road, sea or air. It has branches and agencies throughout the country. The functions assigned to Transpred are performed by the three State Forwarding Enterprises: Despred, Bulfrakht and Inflot. Despred handles international shipments for import, export, transit and re-export of goods by rail, road, sea and air. Bulfrakht is responsible for the freighting of Bulgarian and foreign ship tonnage for the transport of Bulgarian and foreign cargoes by sea and river. Inflot offers agency services to all foreign vessels that call at Bulgarian ports, as well as to all Bulgarian vessels making voyages abroad.

## INSURANCE

Insurance and reinsurance for Bulgaria's foreign trade are undertaken by Bulstrad, the Bulgarian Foreign Insurance and Reinsurance Company, owned jointly by the State Insurance Institute, the Central Union of Co-operatives and a number of State-owned transport and foreign trade enterprises. It handles all types of insurance, including cargo insurance for import, export and re-export of goods, and for property used in fairs and exhibitions.

## VIII. TRADE DOCUMENTATION AND ARBITRATION

### CONTRACTS

Bulgarian FTOs use extensively the standard contract forms devised for different types of transactions, such as export/import of products, technology transfer, licensing arrangements, turn-key contracts, etc. The main body of a form outlines the basic commercial terms of transactions, technical specifications, accompanying services (such as installation and commissioning of the equipment, training of buyers' personnel, etc.), and penalty clauses for late deliveries or delayed performance. The form also includes a comprehensive clause spelling out guarantee obligations. To ensure compliance, Bulgarian FTOs generally insist on inspection before shipment. A force majeure clause is an integral part of every contract.

### ARBITRATION

Contracts with Bulgarian FTOs usually provide for arbitration before the Court of Arbitration of the Bulgarian Chamber of Commerce and Industry. However, they also accept arbitration in third countries, such as Switzerland and Sweden. Bulgaria is a signatory of the European Convention on International Commercial Arbitration, which it signed in Geneva on 21 April 1961.

### DOCUMENTATION

Contracts entered into with FTOs specify the documents required (plus the number of copies of each document), the language(s) acceptable for use in the documents, whether certification and/or legislation may be necessary, and any special certificates that may be required by the contract in question, plus any regulations that must be met for the goods being shipped under that specific contract. Packing, marking and labelling requirements will also be specified. Documentation requirements are usually as follows:

(a)  Airway bill.  Nine copies on standard IATA forms;

(b)  Bill of lading.  No regulation;

(c)  Certificate of origin.  Three copies of general form to be certified by a chamber of commerce.  Two copies to accompany shipment.  Required only on special request;

(d)  Commercial invoice.  Three copies.  State country of origin;

(e)  Consular fees.  None;

(f)  Consular invoices.  None;

(g)  Insurance.  Must be handled in Bulgaria by Bulstrad;

(h)  Marking packages.  No regulations;

(i)  Packing list.  Required;

(j)  Packing materials.  Tin cans or other hermetically sealed containers in which the contents are not visible are prohibited;

(k)  Samples.  Free of duty, if of no commercial value;  and

(l)  Special instructions.  Certificates of disinfection are required for used clothing issued by a medical institution.  Phytosanitary certificates are required for shipments of plants and materials.  Veterinary certificates are required for the import of animals and animal products.

## CHAPTER VII

## TRADING WITH CZECHOSLOVAKIA

### I. ECONOMY

Czechoslovakia is one of the most industrialized countries of CMEA. It is situated in Central Europe with Poland to the north, the German Democratic Republic to the north-west, the Federal Republic of Germany to the west, Austria to the south-west, Hungary to the south-east and the USSR to the extreme east. Its population was estimated at 15.7 million in 1983.

### STRUCTURE OF THE ECONOMY

Czechoslovakia, like any other socialist country, has State ownership of the means of production and planned economic development.

During the period from 1970 to 1983, the growth rates of basic economic indicators were as follows (1970 = 100): gross domestic product (GDP) increased by 166 per cent, national income by 162 per cent, industrial production by 185 per cent, agricultural production by 123 per cent, capital investment by 164 per cent and retail trade turnover by 164 per cent.

The share of industrial activity in total national income in 1983 was 61 per cent. Agriculture is not very important, its share being 8.0 per cent of national income. The major industrial sectors are metallurgy, engineering, building materials, glass and ceramics, leather footwear, food-stuffs, ready-to-wear garments, etc. Czechoslovakia has come to rank among the leading industrialized countries in terms of per capita economic potential and the high standard of living of its population. National income has grown over the years.

Today Czechoslovakia is one of the world's leading per capita producers of steel, iron, electricity, cement, cellulose, sulphuric acid and other industrial products. Its share in world industrial production is 1.7-1.8 per cent - six times greater than its share of world population. It is the second largest per capita producer of coal (after the German Democratic Republic) and the third largest per capita producer of steel (after Belgium and Luxembourg).

The national economic Five-Year Plan now in force (1981-1985) aims at annual economic growth of between 2.0 per cent and 2.6 per cent. Capital investment is targeted to increase each year, on average, by 1.0 per cent, industrial production by 2.7-3.4 per cent, agricultural production by 1.4-1.9 per cent and foreign trade by 6.2-6.9 per cent. Major industries to be accorded high priority are power generation, engineering, chemicals, wood, paper, food-stuffs and consumer goods.

### II. FOREIGN TRADE

Foreign trade plays an important role in the Czechoslovak economy owing to historical and economic factors in the country's development. A small internal market, a developed manufacturing industry, a relatively limited raw material base and dependence on external food supplies are the characteristics of Czechoslovakia's economic life that make foreign trade necessary. Czechoslovakia needs external markets for its manufactured goods and outside sources of supply for raw materials.

By 1982, foreign trade turnover had increased fourfold compared with 1970. This rate of increase was higher than that of industrial production because foreign trade prices increased faster than internal wholesale prices. Trade turnover in 1982 stood at 207 billion dollars, compared with 7.5 billion dollars in 1970.

## COMPOSITION OF TRADE

Czechoslovakia's main exports are metal-working machine tools, textile machinery, tannery equipment, shoe-making machinery, motorcycles, trucks and motor cars, tractors, power generation equipment, electric locomotives, etc. Exports of raw materials and semi-finished products include steel, coal, timber, wood and paper products. Czechoslovakia also exports a number of industrial consumer goods, including textiles, footwear, clothing, linen, glass and ceramic products and furniture.

Machinery and equipment account for 33.3 per cent of total imports, which also include the import of modern technology. Raw materials and fuels represent about 41.1 per cent of total imports, food-stuffs and raw materials for food industry 6 per cent, and industrial consumer goods 6 per cent. The growing share of industrial consumer goods is indicative of rising living standards and demand is concentrated particularly on high-quality products and fashionable goods.

## DIRECTION OF TRADE

After the mid-1950s, the geographical distribution of Czechoslovakia's foreign trade stabilized, with only minor changes taking place in recent decades. The socialist countries of Eastern Europe play a leading role in the foreign trade of Czechoslovakia and, in 1982 their share in its trade turnover was about 70 per cent. In 1982 the share of the developed market-economy countries was around 18 per cent and that of the developing countries 10 per cent. Table 4 illustrates the geographical distribution of trade.

## TRADE WITH DEVELOPING COUNTRIES

The developing countries have emerged as important trading partners. Their share in Czechoslovak exports reached 13.7 per cent in 1982, and their share in imports was about 10 per cent in the same year.

With a few exceptions, the bilateral clearing agreements between Czechoslovakia and developing countries have been replaced by convertible currency payment arrangements.

The Asian countries are Czechoslovakia's leading developing country trade partners, accounting for one half of this trade in 1980. Latin American countries occupy second place, followed by the African countries. In recent years, Czechoslovakia has had a positive trade balance with Asian and African countries and a negative one with Latin American countries.

Its leading trade partners among developing countries are Brazil, Cuba, Egypt, India, the Islamic Republic of Iran, Iraq, the Libyan Arab Jamahiriya, the Syrian Arab Republic and Yugoslavia.

Czechoslovak exports to the developing countries consist mainly of engineering products, in particular various types of machinery and equipment,

Table 4

Geographical distribution of Czechoslovakia's foreign trade,
1970 and 1982

(Value in millions of dollars f.o.b.)

| Geographical distribution | Exports | | Imports | |
|---|---|---|---|---|
| | 1970 | 1982 | 1970 | 1982 |
| Total trade | 3 792 | 15 640 | 3 695 | 15 454 |
| of which: | | | | |
| Developing countries a/ | 531 | 2 151 | 402 | 1 565 |
| Per cent of total | 14.0 | 13.7 | 10.9 | 10.1 |
| Developed market-economy countries | 782 | 2 894 | 916 | 2 949 |
| Per cent of total | 20.0 | 18.5 | 24.8 | 19.0 |
| Socialist countries of Eastern Europe | 2 447 | 10 456 | 2 351 | 10 858 |
| Per cent of total | 64.0 | 66.9 | 63.6 | 70.3 |

Source: UNCTAD, "Trends and policies in trade and economic
co-operation among countries having different economic and social
systems", Statistical annex TD/B/1003/Add.1.

a/ Excluding China.

including complete plants, mining machinery, power stations, and equipment for
the machine-building, metallurgical, oil-processing, textile, leather and rubber
industries. Other export items include industrial consumer goods, semi-finished
products and materials, and chemicals.

Imports from developing countries are mainly traditional items such as raw
materials (ores, cotton, hard fibres, leather, natural rubber) and food-stuffs
(coffee, cocoa, fruit). Imports of industrial products, particularly consumer
goods, have also been rising steadily.

Czechoslovakia is interested in importing processed products from the
developing countries because of its own manpower shortage. Although the birth
rate in Czechoslovakia in the 1970s was among the highest in Europe, it will be
several years before this affects the size of the labour force. The present
trend regarding imports of processed raw materials from the developing countries
is therefore likely to continue for some time. It is Czechoslovakia's declared
intention to import more manufactures from developing countries and, in new trade
agreements with these countries, provision is made for more imports of finished
goods.

## TARIFF PREFERENCES FOR DEVELOPING COUNTRIES

Czechoslovakia is a founder member of GATT. Application of the most favoured nation (MFN) treatment clause by Czechoslovakia is in keeping with the contents of GATT provisions.

Czechoslovakia has offered tariff preferences to developing countries since 1972. In 1978, improvements were introduced which extended tariff preferences to practically all import items by a further 25 per cent, i.e. to 75 per cent of MFN tariffs. Preferential duty-free treatment was granted to all products originating in and exported from the least developed countries.

In 1982 and 1984 further improvements were introduced which enlarged the number of beneficiary countries to 120, 32 of which were least developed countries. The items in the negative list have been reduced to six. Details of the preferential scheme are contained in UNCTAD documents TD/B/GSP/CZECH/2 and TD/B/GSP/CZECH/3. Their summary is as follows:

1.   Product coverage

Preferences are granted in respect of all products, except the following: cigarettes, sugar, some sewn articles of fabrics. Their are no tariff quotas.

2.   Depth of tariff cuts

Czechoslovakia grants tariff reductions of 75 per cent from MFN rates for all products included in the scheme and duty-free treatment to least developed countries.

3.   Rules of origin

Czechoslovakia is the signatory of the "Agreement on uniform rules for determining the origin of goods from developing countries in connection with the granting of tariff preferences under the GSP", which was ratified by five socialist countries granting tariff preferences in 1981.

In order to quality for preferential tariff treatment, the goods eligible for preference must:

(a)   Be despatched directly to Czechoslovakia from the beneficiary country; and

(b)   Comply with the origin criteria specified for those goods.

Goods are considered to have originated in a beneficiary country if they are wholly produced there. If the goods were manufactured wholly or partly from imported materials or parts, those materials or parts must have undergone a manufacturing process in the beneficiary country during which the goods acquired their basic characteristics, and which increased the value of the imported materials or parts by at least 100 per cent.

In this connection, materials or parts imported from Czechoslovakia and subsequently re-exported as part of finished products are considered as originating in the country (donar country content). Czechoslovakia also

considers materials or parts imported from other beneficiary countries and used
in the manufacture of export products as originating in the country (cumulative
origin).

The goods for which preferential tariff treatment is claimed must be
accompanied by a certificate of origin.

### III.  FOREIGN TRADE ORGANIZATIONS (FTOS) - ROLE AND FUNCTIONS

The administrative structure of foreign trade in Czechoslovakia is similar
to that of most socialist countries (see chapter II).  Foreign trade transactions
are carried out by foreign trade organizations (FTOs).  The specific products and
services to be dealt with by each of these corporations are clearly demarcated
by the Ministry of Foreign Trade.  The volume and price of a particular product
purchased or sold abroad by a FTO, as well as the sources of imports and
destination of exports, are determined by FTOs.  These organizations are closely
involved with the Ministry of Foreign Trade in drawing up annual foreign trade
plans and co-operate with the planning authorities in reviewing the progress
of these plans' implementation.

FTOs do vary, however, in status and scope.  The different types are as
follows:

1.  FTOs established by Federal Ministry of Foreign Trade

These deal with specific products/services assigned by the Ministry of
Foreign Trade and are responsible for the exports and imports of those companies/
manufacturing enterprises not authorized to deal in foreign business directly.
KOVO, MERKURIA, etc. come under this category.

2.  Large-scale manufacturing enterprises licensed to do direct business
with foreign countries

These FTOs are, in fact, import/export departments of large industrial
enterprises and licensed by the Ministry of Foreign Trade to transact foreign
business in respect of their own products.  CHIRANA, manufacturing medical
instruments comes under this category.

On 1 January 1983, new forms of economic and organizational linkage between
the production enterprises and foreign trade corporations were introduced on an
experimental basis.  These experiments should provide more effective participation
of the Czechoslovak economy in the international division of labour, closer
linkage of production and foreign trade activities so as to ensure the direct
impact of foreign trade operations on the economic results of production
enterprises.

The first form of the experiment - economic and organizational linkage -
means that those production enterprises having been already earlier authorized to
carry out export activities have now been entitled to handle the import operations
as well in commodity structure which has to correspond to the product-oriented
structure of respective enterprises.  Several important industrial complexes with
comprehensive production programmes have been chosen to test the function of this
experiment.

The second form of the experiment - economic linkage between the production enterprises and foreign trade corporations - means the establishment of the new economic relationship between production and foreign trade.  The previous relationship, when production enterprises had been selling the goods to foreign trade corporations and the latter exported them on their own account, has been replaced by a new relationship where foreign trade corporations carry out foreign trade activities on behalf and on the account of the respective production enterprises on a commission basis.  For this purpose, certain production enterprises with the comprehensive product structure and foreign trade corporations with corresponding export-import commodity structure have been chosen.

In the first case (economic and organizational linkage) the foreign trade organization is organizationally incorporated in a respective manufacturing sector;  in the second case (economic linkage) the foreign trade corporation remains the organizational unit of the foreign trade.

3.    Joint-stock companies with limited liability

These are formed by groups of factories/manufacturing organizations and authorized to carry out foreign business by the Ministry of Foreign Trade. CENTROTEX and EXICO come under this category.

4.    FTOs formed by co-operative enterprises

These are formed by groups of co-operatives engaged in the manufacture of similar products.  The co-operatives are shareholders of these corporations and authorized by the Ministry of Foreign Trade to conduct foreign trade.  These FTOs usually prefer to import from co-operative manufacturing organizations abroad. Most food-stuffs and agricultural products and many simple manufactures are imported directly by these FTOs.  UNICOOP and INTERCOOP come under this category.

5.    FTOs for services relating to foreign trade

These render marketing services of different kinds, including publicity, advertising, market promotion, freight forwarding, commercial representation of foreign firms and the like.  RAPID, MADE-IN PUBLICITY and CECHOFRACHT come under this category.

## FTOS' IMPORT OPERATIONS

Imports into Czechoslovakia are not limited by any quantitative restrictions or licence procedures.  The basic regulatory factors for imports are normal commercial considerations, the availability of foreign currency reserves and, in particular, the potential of export to partner countries.

The foreign trade plan communicated to the respective FTOs by the Federal Ministry of Foreign Trade serves as guidelines for their import programme.  Within the over-all parameters of the import plan, FTOs make the decisions to import.

Foreign exchange is made available by the Commercial Bank of Czechoslovakia in favour of respective internal enterprises or trade organizations for all the envisaged imports and the allocations are not broken down by countries.

The quantities of goods imported have to satisfy the needs of individual branches of the national economy (production, investment, internal trade), taking into account the country's external financial position. Sources of imports are determined on the basis of intergovernmental agreements as well as on the basis of price, quality, terms of trade and other similar consideration of a competitive nature. Allocation of foreign exchange is made to individual trade organizations for a specific trade period (normally one year).

## IV. ECONOMIC CO-OPERATION WITH DEVELOPING COUNTRIES

The fact that Czechoslovakia is able to provide complete industrial installations and produce more than 75 per cent of the various types of machinery manufactured in the world has promoted the expansion of its industrial co-operation with developing countries. Projects carried out in developing countries with Czechoslovak assistance not only help to satisfy domestic requirements, but also provide goods for export to other countries, including Czechoslovakia. The complete industrial installations exported to developing countries include thermal and hydroelectric power stations; factories for the production of building materials (i.e., cement works, ceramic works, etc.); food processing factories such as sugar refineries; engineering works; iron and steel works; textile, leather and footwear factories; and chemical plants, including petroleum refineries.

## V. MARKETING TECHNIQUES AND PROMOTIONAL MEASURES

The organization of FTOs in Czechoslovakia is designed to increase the efficiency of foreign trade operations, since under this system producing and consuming enterprises have more contact with foreign trade partners and a greater say in the formulations of the foreign trade plan.

Usually there is only one competent FTO for any particular foreign trade operation. The buying decision for any major import may involve a number of bodies, including the competent industrial ministry. Although a developing country firm's trade partner will be one of the competent FTOs, it is possible to establish direct contacts with Czechoslovak producing or consuming enterprises. This is especially so in the case of FTOs representing producing or consuming enterprises, and in the case of complex transactions involving industrial licensing and co-operation, when prospective manufacturers, research institutes and other users are involved in negotiations conducted by the competent FTO with a foreign supplier firm. In general, it may be said that the more established a foreign firm is in Czechoslovakia, the better its chance for direct contact with Czechoslovak end-users.

The decision-making process for the majority of Czechoslovak purchases is fairly quick and depends on an evaluation of alternative sources of supply. Transactions providing for mutual exchange of products under a co-operative arrangement, up to a total value of $500,000, can be concluded solely on the authority of the general manager of a Czechoslovak competent FTO. Deals involving a total value between $500,000 and $1.5 million require the approval of the relevant industrial ministry. Deals exceeding $1.5 million in value must be approved by the Federal Ministry of Foreign Trade.

### AGENCY FIRMS AND OPENING BRANCH OFFICES

Commercial representation in Czechoslovakia is possible in one of the following ways:

(a) The engagement of a Czechoslovak agency that has been permitted to represent foreign companies in Czechoslovakia; and

(b) The establishment of one's own trade representation after obtaining a licence from the Federal Ministry of Foreign Trade.

A licence to establish one's own trade representation may be granted only to a foreign company that has developed substantial business with Czechoslovak FTOs. The licence is usually for one year, but can be extended on an annual basis. Foreign companies' trade representatives are expected to confine their business activities primarily to the Czechoslovak agencies established to handle foreign trade. The 11 State agencies under the USOZ—Association, Na strži 63, 140 62 Praha 4 are the following:

1. EFEKTIM         - Capital equipment, including electronics;

2. INTERNAL        - Food products, equipment and consumer goods;

3. MEDIA           - Glass, cermaics, textiles, auto machinery and equipment;

4. INTERSIM        - Machine tools and related equipment;

5. PHOENIX         - Civil engineering machinery, transport and packaging equipment;

6. PRAGENT         - Consumer goods;

7. REPHACHEM       - Chemicals and pharmaceuticals;

8. TRADEX          - Catering gear, hospital equipment and consumer goods;

9. UNIFRUX         - Food and farm products and machinery;

10. ZENIT          - Complete plants and equipment for various industries; and

11. MERCANTA       - Small-scale machines, optics and printing machinery.

The cost of hiring a State agency will depend on the product and range of services to be provided. The agencies ask for a commission on sales. Only State agencies are permitted to handle after-sales service and consignment stock on behalf of a foreign firm.

## TRADE FAIRS AND EXHIBITIONS

The Brno International Fair, organized in September every year, exhibits mainly engineering products. Consumer goods are exhibited at Salimo Brno Consumer Goods Fair, held in April; while Incheba Bratislava has exhibitions of commercial products in June. It is also possible to organize national exhibitions or specialized shows with the assistance of the Czechoslovak Chamber of Commerce and Industry.

## CZECHOSLOVAK CHAMBER OF COMMERCE AND INDUSTRY

The Chamber of Commerce and Industry plays an important role in the country's foreign trade. It represents more than 600 member organizations - FTOs, industrial corporations, research institutions, etc. Its functions and activities are similar to those of chambers of commerce in other socialist countries. It has established close links with chambers of commerce in various developing countries through co-operation agreements. All these agreements contain provisions for the exchange of delegations. In the course of these exchanges, contracts are concluded and the implementation of projects is discussed. Even in cases where no formal co-operation agreements exist, the Czechoslovak Chamber of Commerce co-operates with its counterparts in developing countries.

The Chamber of Commerce consist of seven sections: (a) heavy engineering; (b) chemical, building and mining industries; (c) consumer goods industry; (d) food industry; (e) employers; (f) banking and finance; and (g) maritime and law. In addition, the Chamber has eight independent specialized commissions:

(a) For dealing with problems of foreign trade;

(b) For disseminating technical and economic information;

(c) For uniform control of quality;

(d) For prevention of losses in foreign trade;

(e) For packing;

(f) For publicity and sales promotion;

(g) For telecommunications; and

(h) For standardization and mechanization of work for international trade.

An independent arbitration court is also attached to the Chamber.

### V. QUALITY CONTROL AND INSPECTION

Czechoslovak FTOs have standardized quality definition for exports by adopting national standards. If the norms for any goods do not correspond to the requirements of the world market, reference is made to the appropriate national standards in the contract, with a reservation allowing for improvement in the quality of the goods in question.

The following institutions handle quality control in Czechoslovakia:

1. INSPEKTA undertakes quality and quantity control of goods, in various foreign trade deals. It operates at the request of Czehcoslovak FTOs or a foreign institution for quality control, or at the direct request of a foreign customer. An agreement on quality control operations serves as the legal foundation for INSPEKTA's relations with the customer (such an agreement is regarded as valid on the basis of Law 101 of 1963, which deals with the legal aspects of international commercial relations). INSPEKTA's role is based on its complete neutrality, and the scope and methods of its work are stipulated in the contract. After examination, INSPEKTA issues an appropriate certificate and bears no responsibility for any subsequent defects in goods if these are found after it has carefully examined them in accordance with the established rules. If INSPEKTA requests some other quality control institution to carry out the examination of goods, all responsibility is borne by INSPEKTA. The examination carried out by INSPEKTA is to be paid for on terms stipulated in the contract.

2.    The Institute of Industrial Design.  This is a specialized organization
under the State Commission for Scientific, Technical and Capital Development that
is supposed, among other things, to establish which manufactured articles
considering their social and instrumental significance are more in line with
current developments in industry and consumption.  The Institute assesses
manufactured goods according to their sanitary, aesthetic and other qualities.
Technical parameters are regarded as criteria for listing particular commodities
among the best Czechoslovak products, bearing the seal "Selected for CID"
(Czechoslovak Industrial Design).  An item is so listed if its characteristics, or
those of the model currently in production or to be produced shortly, are of the
highest degree of quality.

## VI.  BANKING SYSTEM

Two banks, the Czechoslovak State Bank and the Czechoslovak Commercial Bank,
play a very important role in the country's foreign trade.  Implementation of the
provisions of the Foreign Exchange Act is entrusted to the State Bank, which, as
the supreme foreign exchange body in the country, is responsible for elaboration
of the foreign exchange draft plan in collaboration with appropriate governmental
bodies, as well as overseeing and supervising its implementation.  The State Bank
is also responsible for granting credits and defining interest rates.  It has the
exclusive right to issue bank notes.  It lays down the principles for granting
and accepting foreign credits and adjusts payment relations at home and with
foreign countries.  It also establishes the official exchange rate.

The Commercial Bank was established in 1965 to help promote and implement
banking, trade and financial policy in foreign trade relations.  It is a joint-
stock company whose stockholders are national legal entities, financial
institutions, large industrial enterprises and FTOs.  Its principal functions
are:

(a)  trading in foreign currencies;

(b)  keeping payments accounts and undertaking banking operations under agreed
payments and credit contracts;

(c)  making payments in transferable roubles through the International Bank
for Economic Co-operation in Moscow;

(d)  carrying out banking relations in the sphere of foreign exchange non-
commercial payments;

(e)  keeping deposits in convertible currencies;  and

(f)  financing and granting credit to FTOs.

The principal instrument guiding the work of the Commercial Bank is the
Czechoslovak foreign exchange plan.  It is also subject to the supervision of the
Ministry of Finance.  The Bank co-operates with the Ministry of Foreign Trade in
drafting international trade agreements and arrangements, especially regarding the
mode of payment and clearance and granting of credit to FTOs.  The Bank has
representatives in France, the Federal Republic of Germany, India, Yugoslavia and
other countries.

## METHODS AND TERMS OF PAYMENT

All the usual terms of payment, ranging from cash payment to long-term credit for 8-10 years, are in use. For urgently needed imports, Czechoslovak FTOs may be willing to pay cash, even if considerable amounts are involved. For other imports, they may insist on credit terms, varying from 90 to 180 days.

Cash transactions are handled on a cash against documents (c.a.d.) basis. The exporter's bank sends the documents to the Czechoslovak Commercial Bank, which pays after receiving them. For imports, FTOs may establish letters of credit with the Commercial Bank, giving the usual conditions of shipment. When exporting plant and machinery, FTOs offer deferred payment credit terms, which may extend up to 8-10 years.

## VII. MARKETING LOGISTICS

### SHIPPING

ČECHOFRACT (Shipping and International Forwarding Corporation) is engaged in forwarding by sea in its own and foreign vessels, chartering of ships and shipping space, representation of foreign shipping and transport companies, and international forwarding by all means of transport.

ČESKOSLOVENSKÁ NAMOŘNÍ PLAVBA (Czechoslovak Ocean Shipping) is engaged in shipment by Czechoslovak vessels and all activities connected therewith, as well as the purchase, sale and chartering of ocean-going vessels and their accessories, rigging and equipment.

### AIR

Goods to be transported by air are handled by ČSA - Czechoslovak Airlines. Direct air cargo services are also offered by Alitalia (from Rome), Finnair (from Helsinki), KLM Royal Dutch Airlines (from Amsterdam), Lufthansa (from Frankfurt) and Pan American (from New York, Boston, Detroit, Washington, Chicago, San Francisco and Seattle).

### TRANSPORTATION

Česmad (Association of Czechoslovak International Motor Transport Operators) provides technical and other assistance to the vehicles of foreign carriers. The Czechoslovak State railways provide transport facilities for transit cargo passing through the country.

### INSURANCE

Insurance facilities of all kinds, including export credit insurance for and on behalf of either the FTOs or the foreign parties, are provided by the State Insurance Company. It also represents foreign companies and has its own representatives in all major trading centres.

## VIII. TRADE DOCUMENTATION AND ARBITRATION

### CONTRACTS

Czechoslovak FTOs use the types of contract generally applied in world trade. These contracts specify the normal standard terms, such as arbitration, sanctions, guarantees, inspection, tests, acceptance of goods, transportation terms, documentary requirements, force majeure, etc.

## ARBITRATION

As in other socialist countries, there is a permanent Arbitration Court of the Chamber of Commerce of Czechoslovakia in Prague. Disputes may be submitted to a Court of three arbitrators appointed from the specific list, which may include foreign nationals. Unless otherwise provided in the agreement, each party chooses one arbitrator from the list. These two then select a third arbitrator to act as chairman. According to the rules of the Arbitration Court, the President of the Court appoints the arbitrators if they are not appointed by the parties. Arbitration proceedings are conducted on the basis of an arbitration agreement following a written statement of claim. Awards are made in writing on a majority decision of the arbitrators.

## DOCUMENTATION

Contracts will specify the documents required (plus number of copies of each document), important points that must be covered by each document, the language(s) acceptable for use in the documents, certificates that may be required for the order in question, plus any regulations that must be met in shipping the goods. Packing, marking and labelling requirements that must be met will also be specified in the covering contract. Facsimile signatures are not permitted on documents. The following are the detailed documentary requirements based on Czechoslovak laws and/or regulations:

(a) Airway bills. Nine copies on standard IATA forms;

(b) Bills of lading. No regulations. May be made out "to order". Original required for custom clearance;

(c) Certificates of origin. Not required, except for wine and wine distillates to be cleared according to MFN treatment;

(d) Commercial invoices. Three copies to be signed by shipper;

(e) Consular fees. None;

(f) Import licence. Required by importer;

(g) Insurance. Can be arranged through ČESKÁSTÁTNÍ POJIŠŤOVNA

(h) Marking packages. No restrictions;

(i) Packing list. Not compulsory;

(j) Packing materials. No restrictions;

(k)   Shipper's export declaration.  Four copies required;   and

(1)   Special certificates.  Imports of animals and animal products must be accompanied by Veterinary Health Certificates showing details of origin, means of transport, form of packaging and type of guarantee.  Narcotics, firearms, ammunition and explosives are subject to the licensing procedures of the Czechoslovak Ministries of Health and Justice.  Imports of plants and vegetable products must be licensed by the Ministry of Agriculture.

CHAPTER VIII

TRADING WITH THE GERMAN DEMOCRATIC REPUBLIC

I. ECONOMY

The German Democratic Republic is bounded to the north by the Baltic Sea, to the west, south-west and south by the Federal Republic of Germany, to the south-east by Czechoslovakia and to the east by Poland. In 1981 it had a population of 16.7 million.

Since it came into existence 35 years ago, the German Democratic Republic has emerged as a modern industrial State, occupying tenth place in the industrialized world and having a well developed agricultural sector. The country's economic policy is designed to bring steady economic development, improved efficiency and scientific and technical progress.

From 1976 to 1980, national income increased by 25.4 per cent, compared to the five-year plan period from 1971 to 1975; in 1983 it rose by 4.4 per cent, and in 1984 it is due to rise by more than 5 per cent. Industrial production rose by 32 per cent in the period from 1976 to 1980 and in 1983 by 4.1 per cent. Retail trade turnover increased by 5.6 per cent in 1983, and real income per capita rose by 80.1 per cent from 1970 to 1983.

The share of industry in national income amounts to more than 70 per cent, that of agriculture to about 8 per cent. The only available raw materials are brown coal, potash and the basic materials for the glass and ceramics industry. Limited quantities of several non-ferrous ores (copper and tin) and natural gas are also extracted. The German Democratic Republic is the world's largest producer of brown coal (278 million tons in 1983), which is its main source of energy. It has a wide and varied industrial base. It produces a wide range of machine tools, automobiles, ships, lorries, textile machinery, printing machinery, and machines for food processing and packing. The chemical, fertilizer and electronics industries have also been developed.

In recent years, management and planning of the national economy have been placed on a new footing by the formation of combines. Combines are economic units formed with the aim of concentrating industrial capacity, thus improving efficiency. They consist of organically integrated enterprises that pooled their resources. The enterprises belonging to a combine retain their legal independence; they are fully responsible for their planning and accountancy activities and also keep their former names. Since the combine management is responsible for all foreign trade activities, the GDR's foreign trade enterprises are subordinated to both the appropriate combines or industrial ministries and the Ministry of Foreign Trade.

There are at present 132 centrally administered combines coming directly under the relevant ministries and 93 industrial combines under county administration 1/ with a total work force of 3 million, i.e. about 37 per cent of the GDR's over-all labour force.

---

1/ As per 31 December 1983.

The current national economic Five-Year Plan (1981-1985) aims at high economic growth rates. National income is to rise by 28 per cent compared to the previous five-year plan period, industrial production is due to increase by 28 per cent. Large-scale modernization and improvement in labour productivity are planned, with emphasis on increasing production of high quality alloy steel, wider use of micro-electronics and industrial robots, production of engineering and electro-technical equipment, further development of the chemical industry, and reduction of dependence on imports of energy, including petroleum.

## II. FOREIGN TRADE

Foreign trade plays a very important role in the economy of the German Democratic Republic, with about one-third of national income being redistributed through foreign trade channels. During the past decade (1970-1981), foreign trade turnover increased much more rapidly (9.8 per cent per annum) than national income or industrial production. In 1982 the volume of foreign trade reached 41.9 billion dollars, with exports of 21.7 billion dollars and imports of 20.2 billion dollars.

### COMPOSITION OF TRADE

Machinery and equipment are the most important export items of the German Democratic Republic. These include electrical engineering equipment, textile machinery, printing machinery, electronic equipment, and machinery for the dairy/food processing and chemical industries. Other export items include fertilizers, chemicals and industrial consumer goods. With regard to imports, more than 60 per cent of the over-all requirements of raw materials are imported. Various foodstuffs and consumer goods are also imported, as well as a great amount of machinery and equipment.

### DIRECTION OF TRADE

The CMEA member countries account for the predominant share of the German Democratic Republic's foreign trade turnover, followed by the developed market-economy countries and the developing countries. During 1970-1982, the share of CMEA member countries fluctuated between 68.9 per cent and 63.3 per cent; but the developing countries' share increased slightly, from 6.7 per cent to 8.2 per cent, while that of developed market-economies rose from 24.4 per cent to 28.5 per cent.

In 1982 the share of developing countries amounted to 10.5 per cent of the GDR's exports and 7.6 per cent of its imports.

Table 5 shows the volume of trade with the different groups of countries.

### TRADE WITH DEVELOPING COUNTRIES

The policy of the German Democratic Republic has been to develop mutually beneficial co-operation on an equal basis with the developing countries. Trade with these countries is based on intergovernmental agreements assuring the continuous supply and purchase of goods and the intensification of economic co-operation. By the end of 1982, the German Democratic Republic had intergovernmental agreements with 62 developing countries.

Table 5

Geographical distribution of the foreign trade of the
German Democratic Republic

(Value in millions of dollars f.o.b.)

| Geographical distribution | Exports | | Imports | |
|---|---|---|---|---|
| | 1970 | 1982 | 1970 | 1982 |
| Total trade | 4 581 | 21 743 | 4 847 | 20 196 |
| of which: | | | | |
| Developing countries a/ | 394 | 2 293 | 310 | 1 546 |
| Per cent of total | 8.6 | 10.5 | 6.4 | 7.6 |
| Developed market-economy countries | 1 011 | 6 316 | 1 304 | 5 537 |
| Per cent of total | 22.0 | 29.0 | 26.9 | 27.4 |
| Socialist countries of Eastern Europe | 3 133 | 12 927 | 3 198 | 12 977 |
| Per cent of total | 68.4 | 59.5 | 66.0 | 64.3 |

Source: UNCTAD, "Trends and policies in trade and economic co-operation
among countries having different economic and social systems", Statistical annex,
(TD/B/1003/Add.1).

a/ Excluding China.

Exports to developing countries consist mainly of machinery and equipment,
especially for transport and communications, electrification, building and
construction, the textile industry, machine building, printing and the processing
of agricultural products. At the same time, licences and know-how have been
transferred for roller-bearings, boring and milling machines, transformers,
hydraulic presses, milking machines, precision and optical instruments, and field
glasses and photographic films.

Imports from developing countries consist mainly of raw materials, including
crude oil, hard coal, rubber, ferrous and non-ferrous metals, phosphate, cotton,
cotton fabrics, protein fodder, vegetable oil, coffee, tea, cocoa, and tropical
fruits. In recent years, the German Democratic Republic has increased imports of
some manufactures and semi-manufactured products such as handicrafts, textile
products, garments, leather goods, shoe-uppers, sanitary fittings and canned food,
and products of mechanical engineering and the automobile industry, and these now
constitute about 40 per cent of total imports.

## TRADE REGULATIONS

As laid down in article 9 of the Constitution, the State has a foreign trade monopoly in the German Democratic Republic. In other words, foreign trade is taken into full account in State planning activities, is managed by centralized State authority - the Ministry of Foreign Trade - and certain economic entities - usually specialized foreign trade enterprises - that have been appropriately authorized by the State are entitled to conclude and fulfil export and import contracts relating to material products and services or to findings and services in science and technology.

The German Democratic Republic does not levy customs duties or other taxes on commercial imports. Duties are applied only to non-commercial goods or certain goods imported by tourists.

## JOINT VENTURES

Joint ventures are commonly established between enterprises of the German Democratic Republic and those of CMEA member States. The German Democratic Republic is also prepared to enter into joint-venture arrangements with firms of other countries if these are clearly advantageous and situated outside its territory.

## III. FOREIGN TRADE ORGANIZATIONS (FTOS)

The GDR's foreign trade enterprises are economic entities charged and authorized by the State to export and import material products and services as well as results, services and benefits ensuring from advances in science and technology. Only one foreign trade enterprise is responsible for the export and import of a particular kind or similar kinds of goods. As exporters and importers serving one or several sectors of industry or the economy, the foreign trade enterprises exercise the State's foreign trade monopoly for the range of goods and services allotted to them.

The foreign trade enterprises are corporate bodies and perform their activities on the basis of the national economic plan using the principles of commercial accountancy, i.e. their economic activities concentrate on achieving commercial gain. They are obliged to include in their plans deliveries and services arising from agreements which are based on international law and international commercial contracts.

Decrees issued by the Government of the German Democratic Republic on the management and practical aspects of foreign trade activities involving the export and import of production-related scientific or technological knowledge govern the activities of the GDR's organizations, combines, enterprises and research institutions engaged in this particular branch of international trade. These legal regulations cover all kinds of relations which involve the taking-out, granting and exchange of licences and are being increasingly referred to internationally under the generic term "transfer of technology". Hence, the term "export and import of scientific and technological knowledge" stands for the transfer in either direction of the results of scientific and technological research and development work for the purpose of their practical application, the granting or receipt of the permission to use patent rights, and the sale or purchase of scientific and technological knowledge which is either protected by patent or for which no patent has been granted.

Agreements concluded in connection with the export or import of scientific and technological knowledge are foreign trade contracts. These are concluded by the competent foreign trade enterprises in their own name on the account of the enterprises importing or exporting the knowledge or on behalf of GDR citizens.

The competence of a foreign trade enterprise is governed by the range of goods and services it normally handles; in other words, know-how and techniques will be imported and exported only by the foreign trade enterprises responsible for the import and export of the corresponding production plant, machine systems, equipment, appliances, etc.

The GDR has no special regulations governing the magnitude of licence fees and the form of payment either as a lump sum or as royalties (licence fees per article), which are mandatory for certain goods or kinds of goods in several countries. Both forms of payment are commonly used in the GDR's licence trade.

The Central Office for International Licence Trade was established jointly by the Ministry of Science and Technology and the Ministry of Foreign Trade of the GDR in order to encourage and promote the export and import of benefits resulting from scientific and technological advances. It services the combines, enterprises, research establishments and foreign trade enterprises engaged in the licence trade as an adviser on commercial and legal questions. The Office is party to bilateral and multilateral agreements and takes part in the work performed by international organizations regarding questions of the international transfer of technology. It also mediates contacts to those potentially interested in taking out or granting licences.

## IV. MARKETING TECHNIQUES AND PROMOTIONAL MEASURES

A number of institutions are engaged in promoting exports and imports and in rendering assistance to foreign trade enterprise and foreign firms. They include the Chamber of Foreign Trade, the Leipzig Fair Office, Interwerbung GmbH and other agencies. These institutions are of particular significance for partners in developing countries who are not acquainted with the market of the German Democratic Republic.

### THE CHAMBER OF FOREIGN TRADE

The Chamber was established in 1952 and has a membership in 1984 of about 1,000 enterprises and institutions, comprising all FTOs and the most important industrial enterprises and combines.

The Chamber provides various services to the enterprises involved in foreign trade. According to its statute, it looks after the over-all interests at home and abroad of enterprises concerned with the German Democratic Republic's market, whether participating or interested in participating in foreign trade relations. The Chamber supports its members in their market-operations, mainly by establishing business-oriented contacts and by propagating the export potential of the GDR's combines. It produces publications for foreign trade partners, describing the country's economic capabilities, selected industrial branches, its member enterprises and their production programmes. It has established mixed Chambers of Commerce Committees and Sections with partners in several developing countries.

## TRADE FAIRS AND EXHIBITIONS

The International Leipzig Fair is the most important foreign trade event in the GDR. It is held every March and September, lasting seven days each time, under the motto "For Trade Open to the World and Technical Progress".

The body responsible for the Fair is a founder member of the Union des Foires Internationales (UFI). This commercial event attracts some 9,000 exhibitors from about 60 countries every spring and some 6,000 exhibitors from about 50 countries every autumn. The net exhibition area covers about 340,000 m2. The fairs are attended by visitors from around 100 countries. The fact that well-known manufacturing enterprises and foreign trade organizations from the socialist countries, numerous firms and economic organizations from the developing countries and leading firms from the industrialized capitalist countries are all present ensures not only that the fair has a distinctly international character but also that the exhibits are of the highest technical standards. The Leipzig Trade Fair thus offers excellent opportunities for brisk business.

Addresses:    Leipziger Messeamt          or      Branch Office
              (Leipzig Fair Office)               Friedrichstrasse 167-168
              Markt 11-15                         1080 Berlin
              7010 Leipzig

## ADVERTISING AND PUBLICITY

Interwerbung GmbH is the company responsible for the German Democratic Republic's participation in fairs abroad and advertising activities in other countries on behalf of its foreign trade enterprises. It also accepts commissions from foreign firms for advertising in the German Democratic Republic. Advertising possibilities include specialized exhibitions, lectures, symposia, conferences and press advertisements. The International Trade Centre in Berlin also provides an opportunity for foreign enterprises to install their representatives on the spot, in order to facilitate the marketing of their goods.

## INTRODUCTORY OFFERS BY EXPORTERS

In order to sell goods to the German Democratic Republic or to any other CMEA member country, developing country exporters must bring products to the notice of appropriate foreign trade enterprises and their officials. In the first instance, a firm may send a letter of introduction to a competent body, including appropriate data concerning the product - i.e., product specifications and export prices. If appropriate, a sample of the product may be sent with the letter of introduction. Exporters, on receiving an encouraging response to their letters, should plan a visit to the country to negotiate the deal. The final sales contract should specify terms of sale, delivery dates, and methods and mode of delivery. Payment terms should also be specified. The contract will usually specify performance guarantees and inspection by Inter-control, in order to ensure that standards have been met. Inspection of imported goods by Inter-control is at the orderer's expense.

## AGENCY FIRMS

Commercial agents can play an important role in promoting exports from developing countries to the German Democratic Republic. A number of firms are officially authorized to act as local agents for foreign companies. Generally speaking, their services are the same as those offered by similar firms elsewhere.

Since 1 September 1978, the Commercial Agents and Brokers Interest Group, Internationales Handelszentrum, Friedrichstrasse, 1086 Berlin, has been responsible for co-ordinating the activities of the officially authorized agencies. The following are those that may be contacted by foreign companies:

1. AGENA — Oil seeds, vegetable oils foodstuffs, meat, fish, fruit, vegetables, juices, wine, coffee, cocoa, tea, tobacco and spices, equipment for health service, education, laboratory installations and pharmaceuticals;

2. INTERVER — Equipment for electrical engineering, scientific instruments, processing and computer engineering, etc.;

3. KONTAKTA — Diesel engines, pumps, etc.;

4. METAMA — Machinery for food production, farming machines, etc.;

5. TRANSINTER — Chemicals, paints, varnishes, fertilizers, paper, timber, etc.;

6. DIREKTIONS BEREICH MASCHINENBAU — Heavy machinery and equipment.;

7. WAMAG — Machine tools, wood-working machines and mechanical tools; and

8. AGRIMA — Agricultural products, foodstuffs and luxury foodstuffs.

## REPRESENTATIVE OFFICES OF FOREIGN FIRMS

The German Democratic Republic permits foreign manufacturing and trading firms to set up their own representative offices in Berlin to perform technical and commercial functions. Permission is granted by the Ministry of Foreign Trade. A foreign firm seeking permission to set up its own representative office should send an application to the Ministry of Foreign Trade enclosing basic information about the company and details of its current and prospective business dealings.

## V.  QUALITY CONTROL AND INSPECTION

The German Democratic Republic's FTOs have standardized quality definition for exports by adopting national standards.  If the national norms for any goods do not correspond to the requirements of the world market, reference is made to the appropriate national standards in the contract, with a reservation allowing for improvement of the quality of the goods in question.

Inter-control, Clara-Zetkin-Strasse 112/114, ensures quality control of all kinds of exported and imported goods.  It operates on a contractual basis.  A contract stipulates the rights of both sides and the cost of the quality control operations.  Inter-control employs competent experts who travel wherever necessary to check that the quality of goods actually corresponds to the requirements stipulated in the contract.  Inter-control has a diversified network of inspecting bureaux across the country.  On agreement with major international quality control institutions, Inter-control sends its experts abroad to perform quality control inspections.  It also carries out laboratory tests, surveying services, etc.  Certificates issued by Inter-control are recognized by banks as documents against which payments may be effected.

Other quality control institutions in the German Democratic Republic are:

(a)  The Board of Standardization, Measuring Equipment and Control of Goods;
(b)  The Ministry of Health;
(c)  Technical Surveillance;
(d)  State Secretariat for Labour and Wages;
(e)  The Board for Nuclear Security and Radiation Protection;  and
(f)  The High Authority for Mining.

## VI.  BANKING SYSTEM

Two Banks, the State Bank and the German Foreign Trade Bank, play an important role in the foreign trade of the German Democratic Republic.  The State Bank issues and manages currency and maintains close contacts with financial and credit institutions in the country.  It keeps all the accounts of the Government and grants short-term and long-term credits to manufacturing enterprises, combines and managing bodies of industry, building, home trade, transport, postal and telecommunications services and other spheres of the economy.  It is authorized to buy and sell foreign exchange, gold and other precious metals.  It operates a network of branches throughout the country.

The Foreign Trade Bank (DABA) is a joint-stock company founded in 1966 and is an integral part of the country's monetary and credit system.  It is responsible for handling foreign exchange transactions connected with foreign trade.  According to its statutes, DABA operates a commercial and non-commercial payments and clearing system with other countries and participates in the usual international banking operations, including deposits and credit banking with customers within the German Democratic Republic and abroad.  It also handles the major part of all financial transactions, commercial and non-commercial, by economic enterprises and private individuals within the country and from other countries.

It supports FTOs in their export business by rediscounting credits granted to their customers abroad.  Similarly, it supports them with credits for obtaining imports.  To handle payments transactions with other countries, DABA maintains relations with more than 800 banks worldwide.

## METHODS OF PAYMENT

The appropriate FTO will normally stipulate the terms of payment.  Letters of credit form the usual basis of trade, although other methods, such as cash on delivery (COD), may be used.  Medium and long-term credit is usually expected for capital goods, while short-term credit is often demanded for other goods.

## VII.  MARKETING LOGISTICS

### SHIPPING

The German Democratic Republic, which - due to its geographical position - is an important transit country, operates an efficient network of sea (including inland), road, rail and air transportation.  The Ministry of Transport manages and co-ordinates State transport policy.

Enterprises within the German Democratic Republic operating maritime transport and those administering ports are grouped in the VEB Kombinat für Seeverkehr and Hafenwirtschaft in Rostock.  VEB Deutfracht/Seereederei is the shipowner and freight broker.  It operates the country's entire merchant fleet.  Under the designation "DSR-Lines", this enterprise operates 21 scheduled services, among them 11 jointly with partners, primarily from socialist and developing countries.  Within the framework of the Baltafrica and Uniafrica joint services, DSR operates scheduled services to East and West Africa and the Red Sea ports.  The German Democratic Republic is an active member of scheduled shipping conferences.  It also operates container ships in a service to the United Kingdom and Finland.

VEB Deutfracht/Seereederei operates a network of agencies throughout the world and has representatives in most important ports and commercial centres. VEB Schiffsmaklerei is the only authorized shipping line agent and clearance broker in the country's ports.  VEB Binnenreederei is the sole carrier for all goods transported by inland navigation.

### AIR

Goods to be transported by air are handled by the national airline INTERFLUG. Agreements concluded with a large number of other airlines ensure smooth air transportation to all countries.  INTERFLUG operates within the framework of regulations of the States across whose territories it passes or in which it lands, stipulations of the Warsaw Agreement and the Hague Protocol of 1955, the air traffic agreements concluded between the German Democratic Republic and other countries, and its own commercial agreements.

## TRANSPORTATION

Goods traffic crossing the borders is handled by VEB DEUTRANS, with the exception of cargo in large containers, which is the responsibility of the transcontainer organization, DDR CONT. In co-operation with the Danish and Swedish railways, railways in the German Democratic Republic operate ferry connections across the Baltic, serving the routes Warnemünde-Gedser to Denmark and Sassnitz-Trelleborg to Sweden, Norway and Finland. The German Democratic Republic is a signatory to the agreement on international railway goods traffic (SMGS) and the international agreement on railway freight traffic (CIM).

Road haulage is operated by 15 nationally owned lorry transport combines. International road haulage is operated within the framework of the CMR Convention on the international carriage of goods by road, the European agreement on international transport of dangerous goods by road (ADR), the TIR (Transit International Routier) Convention, the Agreement regarding the transport of perishable foods (ATP), the Agreement on the work of drivers (AETR) and bilateral road transport agreements.

## INSURANCE

DARAG is the agency that provides insurance cover against the various kinds of risks in foreign trade. Its main operations relate to property and third party insurance, especially of the means of transport (seagoing and river vessels, aircraft), export/import consignments, stored goods, exhibits at fairs and exhibitions, assembly risks and various third party indemnity insurance.

Its general policies also cover insurance of exports for the foreign buyer (insurance on foreigner's account) if, in the export contract, the FTO has agreed to arrange for insurance cover by relevant terms of delivery (e.g. c.i.f.) or other agreements. Insurance cover is offered on the usual international terms and conditions.

DARAG offers insurance protection in the form of erection insurance against the risks involved during the construction of factories or the erection of plant. This form of insurance is available both for plant and factories being effected abroad (i.e. exported plant) and for those being erected in the German Democratic Republic by foreign firms (imported plant). Erection insurance policies covering the erection of plant and factories abroad are concluded with DARAG by the foreign trade enterprises to the account of the purchaser in accordance with the stipulations agreed upon in the contract regarding who is responsible for erection. In the case of imported plant, erection policies are concluded by DARAG with the foreign vendors themselves.

## VII.  TRADE DOCUMENTATION AND ARBITRATION

### CONTRACTS

The law applicable to contractual relationships in foreign trade and other areas of external economy is the International Commercial Contracts Act (ICCA) (Gesetz über internationale Wirtschaftsveträge (GIW)) of 5 February 1976.

Trade contracts are primarily (a) sales contracts, (b) carrying out of work contracts, (c) assembly contracts, (d) rendering of services contracts.

The law does not place restrictions on the parties working out stipulations to meet specific conditions in individual cases so as to serve mutual interests.  In so far as the parties are agreed on applying the laws of the German Democratic Republic and have not made stipulations on specific rights and duties, the International Commercial Contracts Act applies.

## ARBITRATION

The legal basis of foreign trade arbitration in the German Democratic Republic is the decree on arbitration procedures of 18 December 1975.  The Court of Arbitration within the Chamber of Foreign Trade was established for disputes arising from business transactions, including banking, transport and insurance cases, provided its jurisdiction was agreed upon beforehand and at least one of the parties has headquarters outside the country, or if its juridical competence, binding on the litigants, is regulated by intergovernmental agreements.

The arbitration decision reached by the court is based on the law that both parties have earlier agreed should apply, taking into account commercial usage relevant to the case in dispute, and on regulations issued by the court in accordance with the Standard Regulations for Courts of Arbitration at the Chambers of Commerce in CMEA member countries.

## DOCUMENTATION

Since imports are effected by FTOs, the documentation requirements for exporters of each commercial contract are authoritative and definitive for that particular order, irrespective of value and mode of transport used. Contracts will specify the documents required (plus number of copies of each), important points that must be covered by each document, the language(s) acceptable for use in the documents, whether certification and/or legalization may be necessary, any special certificates that may be required for the order in question, plus any regulations that must be met in shipping the goods. Packing, marking and labelling requirements that must be met will also be specified in the covering contract.  Facsimile signatures are not permitted on documents.  The following are the detailed documentation requirements based on the laws and/or regulations of the German Democratic Republic:

(a)  Airway bills.  Nine copies on standard IATA Forms;
(b)  Bills of lading.  No special regulations;
(c)  Certificates of Origin.  Two, unless otherwise specified by the importing FTO.  When required, these must be certified by a Chamber of Commerce;
(d)  Commercial invoices.  No special form;
(e)  Consular fees.  None;
(f)  Consular invoices.  None;
(g)  Import licence.  Required by importing FTO;
(h)  Insurance.  Certificate usually arranged by the importer;
(i)  Marking packages.  Show country of origin, contract number, shipping marks, weight and colis number;

(j) Packing list. Not compulsory. When issued, data should agree with that in other documents, including sales contract number;

(k) Packing materials. No restrictions;

(l) Shipper's export declaration. Required for all shipments; and

(m) Special certificates. Sanitary and health certificates are required for live animals, animal products, pork and sausage products. Flowers, plants and shrubs must be accompanied by a certificate issued by agricultural authorities in the country of origin. An import permit is required for arms, ammunition, explosives and military equipment. Special regulations apply to the import of pharmaceuticals.

Freight and commercial documents should include:

- contract number of importing FTO;

- invoice or specification with value and net weight.

## CHAPTER IX

## TRADING WITH HUNGARY

### I. ECONOMY

Hungary is located in Eastern Europe, bounded to the north by Czechoslovakia, to the east by the USSR and Romania, to the south by Yugoslavia and the west by Austria. Its population in 1983 was estimated at 10.7 million.

During the period 1970-1983, the growth of basic economic indicators was as follows (1970 = 100): Gross domestic product and the national income each rose by 171 per cent, industrial production by 170 per cent, agricultural production by 141 per cent, capital investments by 140 per cent, retail trade turnover by 159 per cent and real income per capita by 142 per cent.

Hungary produces a large quantity of brown and hard coal and some oil and natural gas. It lacks most mineral raw materials with the exception of bauxite.

Industry continues to be a key sector of economic development and growth. Over the last 10 years, it has been further modernized and, together with the building industry, now produces 60.1 per cent of Hungary's national income. The most important industry is engineering, which produces road vehicles, buses, parts and components for engines, electronics, telecommunications equipment, instruments, machines and machine systems, and equipment for the agricultural, food lighting, alumina and paint industries.

The chemical industry has also grown in importance. Light industry comprises a wide scope of production activities and provides 14 per cent of exports, depending largely on imported raw materials. As a result of the modernization of the product structure, several processed and manufactured goods are imported, mainly from developing countries.

The national economic Five-Year Plan (1981-1985) now in force aims at annual economic growth of between 2.7 per cent and 3.1 per cent. Capital investment is targeted to increase each year, on average, by 0.9 per cent, industrial production by 3.5-4.1 per cent, agricultural production by 2.3-2.8 per cent and foreign trade by 4.6-5.4 per cent.

### II. FOREIGN TRADE

Not being endowed with many natural resources, Hungary has to depend to a large extent on international trade. It maintains trade relations with 144 countries.

Over the period 1970-1983 the share of exports in national income has increased from 26.3 per cent to 50.2 per cent. The share of imports in national income has risen even more, from 21.3 per cent in 1970 to 49.0 per cent in 1982.

Total trade turnover increased from 4.8 billion dollars in 1976 to 17.7 billion in 1982. Exports increased from 2.3 billion dollars to 8.8 billion and imports from 2.5 billion dollars to 8.9 billion.

## COMPOSITION OF TRADE

Being increasingly dependent on foreign trade, Hungary has to diversify its markets and products. The major items in exports are steel, textiles, vehicles, and agricultural products. Imports consist principally of machinery and equipment, petroleum, iron ore and coal.

There has been a marked shift in the commodity composition of Hungarian exports to the developing countries, with an increasing share foodstuffs.

## DIRECTION OF TRADE

Table 6 shows the geographical distribution of trade.

Table 6

Geographical distribution of Hungary's foreign trade: 1970-1982
(Value in million dollars f.o.b.)

| Geographical distribution | Exports | | Imports | |
|---|---|---|---|---|
| | 1970 | 1982 | 1970 | 1982 |
| Total trade | 2 317 | 8 852 | 2 505 | 8 861 |
| of which: | | | | |
| Developing countries a/ | 229 | 1 540 | 248 | 1 259 |
| Per cent of total | 9.9 | 17.4 | 9.9 | 14.2 |
| Developed market-economy countries | 630 | 2 652 | 678 | 3 232 |
| Per cent of total | 27.2 | 30.0 | 27.0 | 36.5 |
| Socialist countries of Eastern Europe | 1 440 | 4 626 | 1 562 | 4 340 |
| Per cent of total | 62.1 | 52.2 | 62.4 | 49.0 |

Source: UNCTAD, "Trends and policies in trade and economic co-operation among countries having different economic and social systems", Statistical annex, (TD/B/1003/Add.1).

a/ Excluding China.

Trade with the CMEA member countries has been growing. The share of the socialist countries in over-all Hungarian trade turnover was around 50 per cent in 1982. These countries provide more than 80 per cent of oil and fuel, 50 per cent of raw and basic materials, more than 60 per cent of capital goods and nearly 50 per cent of spare parts. Moreover, 80 per cent of Hungary's exports of machinery and equipment and more than 50 per cent of industrial consumer goods and foodstuffs are delivered to these countries.

The share of the developed market-economy countries in Hungary's total trade was about 33 per cent in 1982.

## TRADE WITH DEVELOPING COUNTRIES

Developing countries have emerged as important trading partners of Hungary. As a result, their share in total trade turnover increased to about 15 per cent in 1982, compared with 9.4 per cent in 1970. At present Hungary has trade and economic co-operation agreements with 86 developing countries. Intergovernmental agreements with these countries provide a framework for economic, commercial, financial and technical co-operation and facilitate the activities of companies by fostering favourable conditions for establishing direct contacts to promote co-operation and business deals. Some of the intergovernmental agreements are trade and payments arrangements and others are agreements on economic, technical and scientific co-operation.

Hungary is in favour of the multilateral system of payments and has shifted away from the clearing system of payments with developing countries. The clearing system is now in operation with only four developing countries.

The commodity pattern of trade with the developing countries corresponds to the structure of production of the Hungarian economy, as well as to development trends in partner developing countries. Hungarian exports consist mainly of machinery, equipment, instruments, vehicles, industrial consumer goods and, in recent years, increasing quantities of agricultural and food products. The most important import items are tropical foods, agricultural products, oil and fuel, while at the same time the proportion of manufactured products and consumer goods is rapidly increasing. Consumer goods from developing countries have become an important factor in the Hungarian domestic market, particularly cotton knitwear, leather products and jackets, garments, sportswear, textile fabrics, carpets and rugs, footwear, electrical appliances, steel products, cosmetics, household articles, sports goods, handicrafts and preserved foods. Hungarian imports also include engineering industry products, machines, tools and spare components for vehicles.

## TARIFFS AND TARIFF PREFERENCES

The structure of Hungarian customs tariffs is based on the Brussels Tariff Nomenclature, since Hungary is a signatory of the Nomenclature Convention established by the Customs Co-operation Council.

The Hungarian system includes about 3,200 tariff headings and subheadings and presently has two columns. The tariff rates of column 1 are applied to goods originating in developing countries that enjoy preferential tariff treatment in Hungary. The tariff rates in column 2 are applied to goods originating in countries with which trade is conducted according to most-favoured-nation (MFN) treatment. According to Hungarian customs regulations, the tariff rate applied to goods from countries that do not accord MFN treatment to Hungarian goods is three times MFN rates. The average rate of customs tariffs in column 2 was 20.1 per cent ad valorem in 1983.

Hungary is a member of GATT. It participated in the Tokyo Round of multilateral trade negotiations and has signed some of the protocols and agreements which provide, inter alia, that the average of the Hungarian MFN rates will be cut to 14.8 per cent by 1 January 1989. In 1981 Hungary became a member of the International Monetary Fund and the World Bank.

In 1972, Hungary introduced a scheme of tariff preferences in favour of developing countries. At present, preferential tariff treatment is accorded to 1,435 products originating in developing countries, including industrial and agricultural goods. The tariff concession granted to developing countries ensure duty-free entry to the Hungarian market for approximately 100 products, while, for other products, MFN rates were reduced by between 50 per cent and 90 per cent. In determining the eligibility of a developing country for preferential tariff treatment, the main considerations are:

(a) Its _per capita_ national income should be lower than that of Hungary;

(b) It should maintain normal trading relations with Hungary without applying discrimination; and

(c) The origin of the product enjoying preferential tariff treatment should be certified.

The preferential tariff system is extended to 92 countries. All products from the least-developed countries enter the Hungarian market duty-free. The Hungarian GSP scheme does not contain any restrictive element. No quota or ceiling is established for the imports of the goods receiving preferential treatment. The average rate of preferential tariffs was 5 per cent in 1983.

Rule of origin. The country where dutiable goods are manufactured or in which they underwent substantial processing is an important factor determining the rule of origin. Substantial processing means that, during processing, the increase in value-added exceeds 50 per cent of the value of the goods. The basis of duty assessed in accordance with the customs tariff is the customs value of the goods, which comprises the total amount of their foreign purchase price plus the costs up to the Hungarian border (freight, insurance, agents commission, etc.).

## III. FOREIGN TRADE ORGANIZATIONS (FTOS)

In Hungary the production, sale, transportation and other services are carried out in large majority by State enterprises and co-operatives. These enterprises and co-operatives are autonomous legal entities, independent both from each other and from the State. They dispose with their own separate property and to the extent of this property they have complete legal responsibilities. Taking into account the profit and other economic interests, it is their exclusive competence to decide how to make use of their capital, what to produce, what and where to sell, what to buy and where from.

In Hungary foreign trade is a State monopoly. Thus, the State creates international conditions for foreign trade by concluding international agreements, establishes the institutional organization of foreign trade, gives authorization to carry out foreign trade activities to the companies and controls this activity. Export and import activities can be carried out only by authorized economic organizations. Economic organizations without authorization can effect exports and imports through the authorized enterprises. In 1984 about 250 enterprises were authorized to engage directly in foreign trade activities, 44 of them were specialized foreign trade companies, the others were industrial enterprises,

State farms and co-operatives.   Authorization to enter foreign trade may be either general or specific, referring in the latter case to the import and export activities of a producing enterprise for own account or to a single transaction or contract.   The import or export of one type of product can be effected through several foreign trade organizations.   The objective of the Hungarian authorities is to improve the institutional framework of foreign trade in order to make it more flexible and better adjusted to the requirements of the international market.

## The import régime

In Hungary all imports and exports are subject to licensing.   The purpose of the licensing system is to ensure that only authorized enterprises engage in import activities and also to monitor statistically the flow of imports and the conclusion of trade contracts.   The objective of the Hungarian authorities furthermore is to pursue a liberal import policy, provided that balance of payments considerations do not prevail and provided that contracting parties do not apply discriminatory trade measures vis-à-vis Hungarian exports.   Hungary is a signatory to the Code on Import Licensing.

## IV.   MARKETING TECHNIQUES AND PROMOTIONAL INSTRUMENTS

### AGENCY FIRMS

To facilitate marketing by foreign companies in Hungary, 10 official commercial agencies have been formed to represent foreign manufacturers.   Their functions are as follows:

(a)  To assist in concluding co-operation deals with Hungarian firms;

(b)  To assist in the drafting of sales contracts;

(c)  To assist in the sale and purchase of licences and technical know-how;

(d)  To assist in providing after-sales service both before and after the termination of guarantees;

(e)  To keep goods on consignment;

(f)  To maintain technical consulting services and co-ordinate advertising programmes;   and

(g)  To assist in setting up displays, workshops, seminars and exhibitions.

The names and addresses of these commercial agencies are as follows:

| | | |
|---|---|---|
| 1. | AGENTURA | - POB 187, H-1368 Budapest; |
| 2. | EUROCOM | - POB 67, H-1441 Budapest; |
| 3. | HUNGAGENT LTD. | - POB 542, H-1374 Budapest; |
| 4. | HUNICOOP | - POB 111, H-1367 Budapest; |
| 5. | IMPORT TRADE | - POB 541, H-1374 Budapest; |

| | | | |
|---|---|---|---|
| 6. | INDUSTRIA LTD. | - | POB 272, H-1117 Budapest; |
| 7. | INTERAG | - | POB 184, H-1390 Budapest; |
| 8. | MERCATOR | - | POB 77, H-141 Budapest; |
| 9. | UNIVERSAL CO. LTD. | - | POB 54, H-1364 Budapest; and |
| 10. | ZENIT | - | POB 164, H-1440 Budapest. |

All the agencies work on a commission basis, the commission charges being comparable with those for the same services elsewhere. These agencies are authorized to establish a special branch (office) for the purpose of representing a foreign trading company. An employee and/or agent of the foreign company is entitled to conduct regular activities in such an office. The conditions for the establishment of such an office will be set out in the approval that must be obtained from the Ministry of Foreign Trade. With the promulgation of the Foreign Trade Act (No. 111 of 1974), trade representation for foreign companies may also be handled by Hungarian economic organizations.

A foreigner living temporarily in Hungary is also allowed to conduct trade activities (including trade representation on behalf of foreign businessmen), without any special permission, with other foreigners and/or with Hungarian enterprises authorized to conduct such activities. Residence will qualify as temporary when the stay of a foreigner in Hungary, on any one occasion, does not exceed three months, or on more than one occasion, a total of six months in a calendar year. Residence in Hungary of less than 14 days will not be considered as temporary residence.

## Industrial co-operation

In Hungary it is the enterprises which decide what co-operation contracts they are to enter into, or whether they are to seek co-operation. Co-operation can be initiated by any company, and co-operation with foreign partners can be established through the intermediary of any company authorized to carry out foreign trade. Naturally, a producing company which has independent foreign trade rights does not need the services of a specialized foreign trade company.

The Hungarian Government supports the enterprises in their endeavours to engage in industrial co-operation, for instance, by the following measures:

- Long-term import and export licences valid for the full term of the co-operation contract;

- Taxation and depreciation benefits for investments in technical development in connection with co-operation contracts;

- Consideration of co-operation contracts as warranties when allocating a special credit line intended for the development of export-oriented production;

- Observation of initiatives for and implementation of co-operation contracts, and special attention to this factor in the evaluation of the performance of enterprise management.

## Economic associations in Hungary with foreign participation

In recent years there has been in Hungary an increasingly serious effort to use, in addition to the manifold development of foreign trade relations, also other ways of international economic co-operation to promote mutual benefits. Various types of co-operation, know-how agreements and patent contracts have spread rapidly.

Associations 1/ are business operations in which a foreign firm, in co-operation with a Hungarian enterprise, establishes a company in Hungary, contributing capital to it. They can have the aim of joint production, of services (hotel, transport, tourism, etc.) and also of carrying out financial activities (banking, etc.). The Hungarian enterprises are mainly interested in associations connected with exports and providing an opportunity to create new profitable capacities.

In an association, Hungarian ownership is minimum 51 per cent, foreign ownership is maximum 49 per cent.

In the banking and service sectors, as well as in other fields, the Minister of Finance may, in specially warranted cases, authorize that the share of the foreign partners be higher. Within these limitations the proportions of ownership may be established freely by the associating partners.

Since 1982 it has been possible to establish economic associations with foreign participation in customs-free zones. These associations are exempt from many of the Hungarian regulations related to other enterprises in Hungary, thus offering more flexible conditions for their efficient operation. Among others, they are not bound by most of the Hungarian foreign exchange rules, the regulations concerning wages and prices, the statutory rules related to foreign trading activity, etc.

There are no customs-free areas specially serving the setting up of joint venture companies. Practically any area, plant or factory can be declared by the competent authorities a customs-free zone (if physical separation is possible) so that investors can flexibly select the proper site for their investment.

### DIRECT REPRESENTATION BY FOREIGN COMPANIES

Foreign firms may be permitted to set up their own trade representation in Hungary, provided that such an agency will develop and promote permanent and fruitful economic co-operation. To obtain such permission, the firm should file a petition containing detailed information about the company and its past relations with Hungarian FTOs with the Minister of Foreign Trade.

---

1/ The notion of an association means an economic association with foreign participation.

The Minister of Foreign Trade ascertains the views of domestic economic organizations through the Hungarian Chamber of Commerce. The decision on an application is communicated within three months.

A representative office of a foreign firm in Hungary has to perform its activities on behalf of the foreign principal in its own name, on its own account and at its own risk. The agency must observe Hungarian laws, especially those concerning foreign trade. It must submit periodic reports on its functioning to the Ministry of Foreign Trade.

The representative office of a foreign firm is allowed to undertake the following activities, unless otherwise specified in the letter of permission issued by the Ministry of Foreign Trade:

(a) To mediate between the principal and Hungarian enterprises in order to conclude contracts;

(b) To act as the confirming house of the principal; and

(c) To provide other agency services, such as the collection of information, arrange advertisements for the principal in Hungarian media, and organize participation of the principal firm in Hungarian fairs, exhibitions, etc.

## SAMPLES AND ADVERTISING

Samples of negligible value are allowed duty-free entry: valuable samples may be temporarily imported duty-free under bond of deposit. A small quantity of printed advertising material is also admitted duty-free. All advertisements in Hungary must be arranged through the following State enterprises:

(a) Advertising Agency. This provides advertising services during the Budapest International Fair and other exhibitions; and

(b) Malur Hungarian Publicity Company, POB 367, H-1818 Budapest. This handles production of commercials, direct mail services, editing and publishing of brochures and catalogues.

## TRADE FAIRS AND EXHIBITIONS

Besides a number of specialized exhibitions, Hungary holds the Budapest International Fair in May and September every year. The May fair exhibits all kinds of investment goods, while the September fair concentrates on consumer goods. For details of participation, developing country exporters are advised to contact the Hungarian Chamber of Commerce, POB 106, Budapest.

## THE HUNGARIAN CHAMBER OF COMMERCE

The activities of the Hungarian Chamber of Commerce centre on representing the interests of its 500 members, which include enterprises engaged exclusively in foreign trade, producing enterprises - some of which are authorized to export and/or import - and servicing and other enterprises. Membership is mandatory for foreign trade enterprises and those authorized to export and/or import, while all others (three-quarters of the membership) have joined voluntarily. The member enterprises account for 85 per cent of total Hungarian trade.

The publications of the Chamber of Commerce (Trade Directory, Information on Hungary, Business Guide in Hungary, etc.) give an accurate picture on the mechanism of imports, on market demands, requirements and conditions.

The publication of Hungaropress gives information on general economic policy issues, on new legal rules and decrees while "Marketing in Hungary" describes the situation and projects of certain branches of the economy, and in this context the possible import demands.

The Hungarian Chamber of Commerce gives assistance to the establishment of business contacts for the enterprises in co-operation with the partner chambers of commerce and industry in the developing countries, by mutual exchange of information and by the publication of business news. Every businessman, trading representative, producer can address himself to the Chamber, asking for the organization of his professional, business programme with the interested Hungarian partners and importers, end-users.

The Chamber also assists Hungarian specialists travelling abroad for the purpose of market research. From time to time, it organizes delegations for this purpose it arranges Hungarian Economic Days abroad and co-operates in the organization of similar events at home, at which Hungarian and foreign partners demonstrate their economic, technological and scientific achievements.

The Chamber maintains contacts with a number of non-governmental international organizations and represents the interests of its members to other chambers and in international organizations of a business federation character. Within CMEA, the Chamber participates in the conferences of chamber presidents and in the conferences of the Arbitration Courts and Corporations of Loss Assessors.

## V.  QUALITY CONTROL AND STANDARDS REQUIREMENTS

Hungary has two types of quality standards:  (a) national standards and (b) company standards.  National standards are laid down by the National Office for Standards, which is under the direct control of the Council of Ministers. Numbering more than 9,000, they are binding for every section of the national economy and are indicated with the letters MSZ.

The national standards are laid down in conformity with the stipulations and norms of the International Standards Organization (ISO), the International Electrotechnical Committee (IETC), the United Nations Economic Commission for Europe (ECE), the Food and Agriculture Organization of the United Nations (FAO), the World Health Organization, etc.

In addition to the national standards, there are about 4,000 branch standards laid down by different ministries and industries, identified by putting two-digit code numbers after MSZ, e.g., MSZ 05.

Departure from either the national or the company standards, which are primarily meant to protect life and health, safe labour conditions, safe transportation, and the interests of individual consumer, is not permitted unless written approval from the authority issuing the standard is obtained. Contracting parties may, however, depart from the stipulations of other State standards, providing such a departure does not jeopardize health and safety protection or the interests of the consumer.

The Ministry of Foreign Trade, with the help of the National Office for Standards, controls the use of standards in foreign trade.

As a general rule, however, Hungary permits the import of commodities which conform to the standards of the manufacturing companies and which possess a quality certificate to that effect.

Hungarian national standards are applied to export products only if a stipulation to this effect has been incorporated in the trade contract with a foreign buyer. However, it is permissible to conclude trade contracts with reference to the standards of any other country, or of the companies, or even to a detailed technical specification. The underlying principle is that Hungarian manufacturers shall be in a position to produce and export their products in compliance with the buyer's wishes.

## QUALITY CONTROL

To enforce the quality standards evolved by the National Office for Standards, Hungary has set up an organization called the Quality Control Company, MERT, under the Ministry of Foreign Trade. This company has been entrusted with the quality control of Hungarian exports and imports, as well as goods passing through in transit. MERT performs quality control functions both at home and abroad and is authorized to appoint the foreign controlling company.

MERT is a fully independent organization whose activities are not influenced by any industrial, commercial or other interests. It works for both domestic and foreign companies for a fee calculated on the basis of the time and wages involved, in accordance with international practice.

There are two other quality control organizations:

(a) KERMI, Commercial Quality Control Institute
József Kert 6
Budapest-VIII; and

(b) MEEI, Hungarian Electro-technical Control Institute,
Váci ut 48a-b
Budapest XIII.

KERMI, under the Ministry of Home Trade, performs compulsory quality control of newly introduced consumer goods, irrespective of whether they have been manufactured by a domestic factory or imported. It also supervises and decides on general complaints or claims lodged by the public. MEEI, under the Ministry of Metallurgical and Machine Industry, controls the quality of domestic manufacturing as well as the importation of electrotechnical products and spare parts, including electro-industrial products.

## MARKING OF PACKAGES

Packages should be marked to show:

(a) Number of the contract;

(b) Number of the customer's instruction;

(c) Number of the import licence;

(d) Serial number of packages;

(e) Gross and net weight;

(f) Addresses; and

(g) Container marks, if any.

Cases/bales must be marked on the two vertical sides. In the case of machinery and equipment, a fraction may be applied in numbering packages - the numerator showing the serial number and the denominator the number of total packages in the shipment.

## VI. BANKING SYSTEM

In Hungary the most important banks are the National Bank of Hungary, the Hungarian Foreign Trade Bank and the National Savings Bank. The National Bank takes part as a member in the activities of the International Bank for Economic Co-operation and the International Investment Bank in Moscow. It is a shareholder in the Bank for International Settlements in Basel, Switzerland. It owns the Central Wechsel and Kreditbank AG in Vienna and the Hungarian International Bank in London, and has representatives in Paris, New York and Zurich. It also has correspondent banking relationships with about 2,000 banks throughout the world.

The National Bank acts as a bank of issue and as a commercial bank. It extends short-, medium- and long-term credits and keeps accounts for the State, State organizations and enterprises, and for co-operatives and social organizations. It is the central organ for co-operative foreign exchange management and for the foreign exchange monopoly, and is also the foreign exchange authority with universal competence.

The Foreign Trade Bank, whose capital was subscribed by Hungarian foreign trade companies, is a joint-stock company. On the basis of its general authorization to act as a foreign exchange bank, it carries out all banking operations connected with foreign countries or firms and may establish subsidiaries abroad. It extends credits to Hungarian enterprises and, in certain cases, will share their risks.

The National Savings Bank has been established to facilitate household savings. Under a special scheme, it also provides interest-bearing foreign exchange accounts in Hungary for foreign nationals. The interest is paid in convertible currency.

## PAYMENT TERMS

Payment terms are usually in accordance with international practice. Certain products, such as machines, plant and equipment, are sold on credit granted for a period greater than one year. In the Hungarian export credit system, loans to foreign buyers may be granted either by the State directly (usually at an intergovernmental level) or by Hungarian enterprises for a maximum period of up to 12 years. Export credit facilities are available to Hungarian companies for such deals. Companies may conclude insurance contracts with the State Insurance Company to cover all internationally acknowledged risks, such as non-payment, exchange rate fluctuations, etc.

For imports into Hungary, payment terms are negotiated during the drawing up of the contract. Payment may be made either on the basis of a letter of credit from the Foreign Trade Bank on the basis of sight or by usance bills. Hungarian companies are empowered to negotiate and conclude contracts on terms mutually agreed with foreign parties.

## VII. MARKETING LOGISTICS

### SHIPPING

In accordance with the principle of the State monopoly of foreign trade, agreements and contracts with foreign railway, shipping and airline companies, as well as with other transport (carrier) agencies, may be concluded only by MASPED, the Hungarian General Forwarding Agents, founded in 1948 specially for performing these tasks. MASPED maintains a widespread network of transport services covering the whole of Europe. Through contracts with international forwarding companies, its activities, in fact, embrace the whole world.

MASPED's activities include international forwarding by road, rail, sea, river and air to and from the most important European cities, as well as Turkey, the Islamic Republic of Iran, Iraq and Kuwait; transit forwarding across Hungary by rail, road or a combination of the two, and on the Danube; leasing of containers and tank wagons; and storage of transit goods or group cargoes in its large bonded warehouses in Budapest's Cespel Free Port.

MAFRACHT, the Hungarian Shipping Agency, is the representative of the Hungarian shipping company MAHART for foreign clients, but also acts as the representative of foreign liner companies in Hungary. In addition, it is responsible for booking shipping space on behalf of both domestic and foreign partners, and for concluding charter parties on the same basis.

MAHART provides the following services:

(a)  Shipping on the Danube from Regensburg to Sulina;

(b)  Maritime shipping in the Black Sea and Mediterranean areas, as well as to Western Europe, South America, India and Singapore;  and

(c)  Loading, storing and clearing of goods (including bonded), container terminals, unloading of containers, reforwarding by rail and road, and from warehouse to warehouse.

## AIR

Malév, the Hungarian Airline, carries air cargoes by scheduled or chartered flights.  Air France, Alitalia, British Airways, Finnair, Iberia Airlines of Spain, JAT Yugoslav Airlines, KLM Royal Dutch Airlines, Lufthansa, PANAM, Scandinavian Airlines System and Swissair also offer cargo service to Hungary.

## TRANSPORTATION

RABERSPED is authorized to act as an international forwarding agency.  It also offers bonded warehouse services at the railway station in Sopron.

HUNGAROCAMION, the International Road Transport Company, arranges international transport of cargoes by normal and special lorries.  It maintains regular services to Hamburg, Rotterdam and other European centres;  undertakes the carriage of goods destined for fairs and exhibitions;  and carries deep-frozen foodstuffs in refrigerated vehicles.  The company is also authorized to act as an international forwarding agency within statutory limits.

## INSURANCE

Állami Biztositó, the Hungarian State Insurance Company, offers insurance cover for operations connected with foreign trade, including marine insurance and export credit insurance.  It also offers other kinds of insurance cover, such as accident and luggage insurance, motor insurance, etc.  Its operations are conducted from its head office in Budapest and its branches throughout the country.

## VIII.  FOREIGN TRADE DOCUMENTATION AND ARBITRATION

## CONTRACTS

Intra-CMEA trade is governed by the General Terms of CMEA Deliveries.  In trade with non-socialist countries, Hungarian FTOs apply the contract terms generally used in world trade.  These contracts specify the usual standard terms, including force majeure, arbitration, sanctions, guarantees, inspection tests, acceptance of goods, transportation terms, documentation requirements, etc.

## ARBITRATION

Hungary has an Arbitration Court attached to the Hungarian Chamber of Commerce. When provided in the contract, disputes are referred to a court consisting of three arbitrators, selected from a panel of 34 people elected annually by the Chamber of Commerce. One of the members is elected chairman. However, parties may decide to use only one arbitrator. The foreign party may choose an arbitrator not on the panel and not necessarily a Hungarian national. Awards are enforced in Hungary by the Central District Court of Budapest. Foreign awards are enforced in accordance with the United Nations European Arbitration Convention and the 1920 New York Convention.

## DOCUMENTATION

Since imports are effected by FTOs, the documentation requirements for exporters of each commercial contract are authoritative and definitive for that particular order, irrespective of value and mode of transport used. Contracts will specify the documents required (plus number of copies of each), important points that must be covered by each document, the language(s) acceptable for use in the documents, whether certification and/or legalization may be necessary, any special certificates that may be required for the order in question, plus any regulations that must be met in shipping the goods. Packing, marking and labelling requirements that must be met will also be specified in the covering contract. Facsimile signatures are not permitted on documents. The following are the detailed documentation requirements based on Hungarian laws and/or regulations:

(a) Airway bills. Two copies;

(b) Bills of lading. No regulations;

(c) Certificates of origin. Two copies on general form, to be certified by a Chamber of Commerce;

(d) Commercial invoices. Three. Must be signed by shipper. No consular legalization required. The commercial designation of goods should be close to the classification of Hungarian customs tariffs. Also state value both in figures and letters;

(e) Consular fees. None;

(f) Consular invoices. None;

(g) <u>Marking packages</u>.   Packages should be marked to show (a) contract number, (b) number of customer's instruction, (c) number of import licence, (d) serial number of packages (if more than one), and (e) gross and net weight;

(h) <u>Packing materials</u>.   No restrictions;

(i) <u>Shipper's export declaration</u>.   Required;

(j) <u>Special certificates</u>.   Sanitary certificates are required for livestock, plants, seeds, etc.   Consular legislation is not required;   and

(k) <u>Insurance</u>.   Usually arranged by the Hungarian importer through the State Insurance Company.

## CHAPTER X

## TRADING WITH POLAND

### 1. ECONOMY

Poland is located in Eastern Europe, bounded to the north by the Baltic Sea, to the west by the German Democratic Republic, to the south by Czechoslovakia and to the east by the USSR. Its population in 1983 was 36.7 million.

The Polish People's Republic is a socialist country with public ownership of the basic means of production. In 1983, 80.4 per cent of the national product was generated by the State-owned and co-operative economy, and 18.5 per cent by the non-socialist economy. The situation in agriculture is quite different, however, with the share of private ownership of the means of production amounting to 80.3 per cent. Economic development follows the course set out in the national plan.

Economic difficulties experienced by Poland in recent years have been caused by complex factors. Investment during the 1970s did not have the expected effect on the production of goods. As a result, the national income index (1970 = 100) diminished from 169 in 1980 to 147 in 1981. At the same time, the share of industry in national income fell to 42.5 per cent in 1981 and that of agriculture rose to 29.9 per cent. However, the national economy is now recovering. The national income index (1970 = 100) increased to 149 in 1983.

In August 1982, the Council of Ministers approved the projections of the Three-Year Economic Plan for the period 1983-1985, as well as preliminary projections for 1986-1990. The main task of the Three-Year Plan is to overcome the crisis and restore economic balance, as well as to complete economic reform.

National income is expected to grow by 11-18 per cent, i.e., at an annual rate of 3.5-5.6 per cent. This means that, in 1985, it will represent 82-87 per cent of its 1978 level, the best year to date. Industrial output should increase by 12-17 per cent over the years 1983-1985. Agricultural production is expected to grow by 6-12 per cent. Changes in the pattern of output will be accompanied by changes in the pattern of foreign trade, resulting from the strengthening of economic co-operation and consolidation of integration with CMEA member countries. Participation by the socialist countries in completing halted investment projects and utilizing idle industrial capacity will also be increased. Another projection is for the developing countries' share in Polish foreign trade turnover to rise from its present 12 per cent level to 15-18 per cent in 1990.

Poland is one of the CMEA member countries that are relatively rich in mineral resources, with deposits of coal, sulphur, silver, copper and lead.

### II. FOREIGN TRADE

The Polish economy, despite its quite plentiful natural resources and large domestic market, is dependent to a large extent on foreign trade for economic growth, as well as for its economic stability. The index of export and import volume (1970 = 100) increased to 197 and 168 respectively in 1983.

## COMPOSITION OF TRADE

Considerable changes have occurred in the commodity structure of Polish foreign trade as a result of industrialization.  In particular, the share of machinery and other industrial equipment (complete industrial plants, ships, cars, machine tools, internal combusion engines, etc.) in exports has expanded from 34.4 per cent in 1970 to about 50 per cent in 1983.  On the other hand, the share in exports of primary goods and material for production decreased from 34.0 per cent to 23.0 per cent in the same period.  Despite these changes, coal remains the biggest single commodity in Polish exports (35.1 million tons in 1983).  The next most important items on the export list are industrial products, namely complete industrial plants, ships, cars and spare parts, clothing, pharmaceutical products, machine tools and internal combusion engines.  The share of manufactured products has risen from 45.2 per cent to about 70 per cent in 1983.  Poland is also an important importer of primary products and manufactured goods.  The share of primary and agricultural products in total imports was 57.0 per cent in 1983, while that of machinery and industrial equipment was 30.0 per cent.

## DIRECTION OF TRADE

Table 7 shows the geographical distribution of Poland's trade:

Table 7

### Geographical distribution of Poland's trade, 1970 and 1982
(Value in millions of dollars f.o.b.)

| Geographical distribution | Exports | | Imports | |
|---|---|---|---|---|
| | 1970 | 1982 | 1970 | 1982 |
| Total trade | 3 548 | 11 215 | 3 607 | 10 254 |
| of which: | | | | |
| Developing countries a/ | 354 | 1 848 | 276 | 857 |
| Per cent of total | 10.0 | 16.5 | 7.7 | 8.4 |
| Developed market-economy countries | 1 024 | 3 731 | 938 | 3 203 |
| Per cent of total | 28.9 | 33.3 | 26.0 | 31.3 |
| Socialist countries of Eastern Europe | 2 141 | 5 531 | 2 369 | 5 990 |
| Per cent of total | 60.3 | 49.3 | 65.6 | 58.5 |

Source:  UNCTAD, "Trends and policies in trade and economic co-operation among countries having different economic and social systems", Statistical annex, (TD/B/1003/Add.1).

a/  Excluding China.

Poland is one of the biggest trading partners of CMEA member countries. The share of socialist countries in its over-all trade is more than 50 per cent, of both exports and imports. Trade with developed market-economy countries has also been substantial, their share in Polish imports and exports being about 30 per cent.

## TRADE WITH DEVELOPING COUNTRIES

Developing countries have emerged as important trading partners for Poland. During the period 1970-1981, their share in Polish exports increased from 9.2 per cent to 13.1 per cent, while their exports to Poland stabilized at about 7 per cent.

As regards the composition of Poland's trade with developing countries, primary products constitute a very important proportion of imports. Their share in total imports from developing countries was no less than 91 per cent in 1980. The share of manufactures in imports was about 8 per cent in the same year. Of total Polish exports to developing countries in 1981, the share of manufactures was 28 per cent and that of machines and transport equipment, 43 per cent.

The present trend towards gradually increasing mutual trade can be expected to continue. Poland currently maintains trade relations with the majority of the developing countries in Africa, Asia and Latin America. The volume of trade with individual developing countries depends on a wide variety of factors, including transport facilities, the availability of specific commodities requested by trading partners, and knowledge of each other's markets.

Poland's major exports to developing countries are engineering products, particularly complete industrial plants and equipment for power-generating stations, for coal and other forms of mining, and for the chemical and food industries. These exports are usually included in intergovernmental agreements on industrial co-operation which, in addition, provide for technical assistance, transfer of technology and other services by Poland. The growing emphasis on international co-operation, which is a constant feature of Polish relations with developing countries, and the recent growth of joint ventures with developing countries, will provide further stimulus to Polish exports of such products.

Changes are also expected in the structure of industrial production, creating conditions for increased co-operation with developing countries by concentrating on products most needed by them (engineering goods, chemicals, etc.) and simultaneously slowing down investment in sectors that enjoy more favourable production conditions in the developing countries (e.g., light industry).

Poland is rapidly becoming an important market for developing countries' exports. Imports of developing countries' primary materials (fodder, gas, oil, phosphates, ores, metals, rubber, textile fibres, hides, etc.) are expected to grow considerably as a result of Poland's increased internal production. There are also good prospects for a shift away from raw materials to more semi-manufactured products in purchases from the developing countries (superphosphates, semi-manufactured textile products, concentrates of ores, etc.). Machines and equipment have, until now, represented only a small proportion of Poland's imports from developing countries. With growing industrial co-operation, however, developing countries might become substantial suppliers of certain goods.

The development of trade and economic relations between Poland and developing countries is based on bilateral trade agreements, long-term agreements on mutual supply of goods, long-term agreements on economic co-operation as well as arrangements related to industrial co-operation in the fields where Poland represents an advanced level of technology and know-how. The bilateral character of such accords does not determine the form of settlement, which can be by either bilateral clearing or multilateral means - i.e. payments in convertible currencies.

In most cases Poland has made arrangements with developing countries under which payments are made in convertible currencies. However, in response to requests made by some developing partners, Poland has also entered into clearing agreements, although in 1984 they represented only 7 out of the total of 55 trade agreements with developing countries.

New efforts are now being made by Poland to expand its trading relationship with developing nations. For example, only in 1984 comprehensive trade were undertaken at the governmental level with more than 20 such partners.

In 1983 a UNIDO Office for Promotion of Industrial and Investment Co-operation with developing countries was established in Poland. Its main task is to assist these countries in their industrialization efforts.

## SCHEME OF TARIFF PREFERENCES

Poland is a member of GATT. It has a customs tariff for commercial imports, introduced in 1976, based on the Brussels Nomenclature. Under the Generalized System of Preferences (GSP), Poland has offered 50 per cent preferential duties or zero duty on many products. As a result, exports from developing countries of some manufactured items have grown significantly.

## III. ROLE AND FUNCTIONS OF FTOs

FTOs and other enterprises normally carry out business in accordance with guidelines laid down by the Ministry of Foreign Trade, which is responsible for the implementation of foreign trade plans and trade policy. They conduct their activities independently, concluding and executing contracts and transactions within the framework of foreign trade plans and trade agreements currently in force with foreign countries.

According to the new economic reform introduced in 1981-1982, the central authorities (Planning Commission and ministries) have been establishing general principles in conducting foreign trade relations and determining the basic tools for regulating external trade operations. FTOs and other trading enterprises have a high degree of autonomy, including their right for independent planning and organization of economic activities. However, the central authorities may influence the decision-making process at the enterprise level by various economic and financial means. FTOs and other enterprises are obliged to respect international and multilateral rules concerning the licensing of imports and exports, as well as the monetary regulations. Such parameters determine the boundaries within which FTOs and other enterprises are free to conduct foreign trade operations according to their own assessment of developings in international and external markets, so as to achieve optimum economic results.

Under the new regulations, enterprises wishing to conduct foreign trade operations obtain a general concession (franchise) from the Ministry of Foreign Trade, provided their export or import activities are compatible with existing foreign trade regulations. There are only a few cases in which it is not possible for individual enterprises to obtain the necessary permission. These involve the export or import of commodities of special importance to the national economy (fuels, grain and some raw materials). The following enterprises are eligible to conclude foreign trade contracts: specialized foreign trade enterprises operating under the Ministry of Foreign Trade; State industrial and other enterprises having the right to trade with foreign partners; co-operative enterprises in the fields of industry, services and trade; companies based on joint ventures utilizing mixed foreign and Polish capital (these enterprises may operate in State, private or co-operative sectors); and private enterprises.

An important new provision allows enterprises engaged in production for export to retain a considerable proportion of their export earning (up to 50 per cent) for the purpose of export expansion. These funds may be freely utilized for the purchase abroad of raw materials and other inputs to increase export production. Under these conditions, exporting enterprises are also becoming importers. This considerably increases the scope of their activities and presents new possibilities for the expansion of trade links with foreign markets and, _inter alia_, with developing countries.

The reorganization of Poland's system of foreign trade is expected to play an important role in the expansion of direct trade links between Polish State, co-operative and private enterprises and their foreign partners. This is particularly important for developing countries, where enterprises involved in foreign trade are usually small compared with those in developed market-economy countries. The reorganization might also be conducive to development of various forms of industrial co-operation of a scale and technological standard suited to the economies of developing countries.

FTOs are highly specialized trade agencies. It is fair to say that, once a FTO has established a business relationship with a foreign supplier that is found mutually satisfactory, the supplier will receive preference when offers are requested. Factors that may affect a long-term relationship include normal commercial considerations and shifting trade patterns in international markets that usually result in price changes. Requests for submission of offers are automatically made to all foreign suppliers of a particular product known to the FTO. A request contains important specifications concerning the products sought. A newcomer should not be deferred by this. He can take the initiative in informing the FTO of his product profile, delivery schedule, prices, etc. Before making a visit to any FTO's office in Poland, it is advisable for the new exporter to make all possible contacts with Polish trade representatives in his own country.

## IV. MARKETING TECHNIQUES AND PROMOTIONAL INSTRUMENTS

The legal rule of State monopoly of foreign trade is exercised at the discretion of FTOs and other authorized enterprises within the general guidelines administered by the Ministry of Foreign Trade. Normally, such enterprises serve as intermediaries between Polish buyers and/or sellers and foreign commercial entities, according to the instructions from the domestic clients. In some cases FTOs buy and sell at their own risk and account. Foreign trade dealings of FTOs and other franchised enterprises are normally guaranteed by the Bank Handlowy. The Polish State is not responsible for their obligations.

At present, an increasing number of foreign trade enterprises enter into direct partnership with industrial entities in order to set up limited liability companies.

For successful trading and maintaining regular contacts with end-users, it is necessary to be properly represented in Poland. This can be done either by appointing one of the authorized Polish commercial agency enterprises or by establishing one's own information and servicing office. All the agencies are located in Warsaw, with branches in major industrial towns. They represent foreign firms on the basis of long-term agreements for a stipulated commission, the rate of commission depending on international practice. These enterprises undertake to:

(a) Provide information on the Polish market;

(b) Perform advertising and market research;

(c) Provide technical guidance on imported goods;

(d) Maintain technical services;

(e) Organize and maintain consignment stores;

(f) Organize and maintain model shops, exhibition shops, fair stalls and specialist exhibitions;

(g) Attend to matters connected with attestation and admission of foreign goods (e.g., pharmaceuticals and electro-engineering products) into the Polish market;

(h) Assist clients' representatives visiting Poland with all administrative matters connected with their stay; and

(i) Organize meetings between clients or their own experts and representatives of Polish industry, foreign trade firms and other users of imported goods.

The addresses of these agencies are:

1. MACIEJ CZARNECKI & CO., LTD., P.O. Box 205, 00-950 WARSAW
2. DYNAMO, P.O. Box 30, 00-950 Warsaw;
3. EXIMPOL, S.A., P.O. Box 810, 00-950 Warsaw;
4. MUNDIAL, P.O. Box P.6, 00-950 Warsaw;
5. POLCOMEX, S.A., P.O. Box 478, 00-950 Warsaw;
6. POLIGLOB, S.A., P.O. Box 40, 00-950 Warsaw;
7. TIMEX, S.A., P.O. Box 268, 00-950 Warsaw;
8. TRANSACTOR, S.A., P.O. Box 276, 00-950 Warsaw;
9. TRANSPOL, S.A., P.O. Box 280, 00-950 Warsaw;
10. UNITEX, S.A., Box 404, 00-950 Warsaw.

Foreign firms, mainly industrial enterprises, may be permitted by the Minister of Foreign Trade to establish their own information or servicing offices in Poland.  Such offices are entitled to undertake only the following activities:

(a)  To provide technical information and services to Polish organizations; and

(b)  To maintain stores of spare parts for goods imported by Poland.

Permission for a foreign firm to open an information/servicing office depends mainly on its past contacts with the Polish market and the possibility of industrial co-operation agreements being signed between the firm and Polish trade and industrial enterprises.  In practice, most foreign firms wishing to assure themselves of full commercial and technological services not only obtain licences to run their own service offices, but also appoint commercial agencies to represent them.

It should be noted that all other forms of commercial agency activity - i.e., other than those through Polish commercial agencies and authorized information/ servicing offices - are prohibited.

## DIRECT REPRESENTATION BY FOREIGN FIRMS

Under decree No. 63 of 6 February 1976, foreign firms may be permitted by the Minister of Foreign Trade to establish and operate their own commercial representation offices in Warsaw or other principal centres of activity in Poland. The decision to grant such permission will depend on a foreign company's current and prospective volume of trade and co-operative arrangements with Poland.  Foreign firms must make a written application to the Minister of Foreign Trade, giving the following information:

(a)  An abstract from a commercial register with data on the firm;

(b)  A declaration by the management of the company's intention to establish representation in Poland;  and

(c)  A declaration stating that the firm's representatives will observe Polish laws.

These documents must be submitted with Polish translations and notarization by a Polish Diplomatic Mission or Consumer Office in or near the parent company's home country.

The accredited representative office of a foreign company in Poland must meet the following requirements:

(a)  To maintain its bookkeeping and accounts in the Polish language and in Polish currency;

(b)  To pay Polish taxes and fees on time;  and

(c)  To maintain an account at the Bank Handlowy, S.A., in Warsaw and settle all accounts and payments in accordance with Polish currency regulations.

Licences for foreign accredited offices are issued for a period of two years and are renewable. The foreign offices may employ Polish nationals who have been granted employment permits by the local authorities. Foreign nationals intending to work in these offices must obtain a permit to work in Poland.

A foreign firm's representative office may take one of the following forms:

(a) A commercial office to undertake activities such as contract signing, consignment storage, sales promotion, etc. Such an office is subject to Polish taxation as regulated by the Ministry of Finance;

(b) A technical information office to provide services such as publicity and scientific research. Such an office is not authorized to conduct any commercial activities; and

(c) A supervisory office. Only foreign firms involved in turn-key projects or industrial co-operation are allowed to open such an office. The performance of either commercial or technical information services is not permitted.

A foreign company's accredited commercial office is liable to pay tax on profits accruing from its turnover in Poland. Taxable profits are determined on the basis of the company's total transactions in Poland, regardless of where the contract was concluded or the role of the representative office in concluding the contract. Taxable profits are either calculated on the basis of the company's accounting books or are the following percentages of total turnover:

(a) Five per cent of total contract value for sale of commodities and equipment;

(b) Ten per cent of turnover for construction and assembly work; and

(c) Sixty per cent of turnover resulting from commission.

Foreign employees of a representative office in Poland are liable to pay Polish personal income tax.

## TRADE FAIRS AND EXHIBITIONS

The Poznan International Fair, held in June every year, is the most important trade fair organized in Poland. Foreign participation is mainly organized on a national basis. Developing country exporters wishing to participate should contact the Polish Chamber of Foreign Trade, which is responsible for organizing the fair.

## ADVERTISING

Advertising in Poland is becoming increasingly important, particularly for technical products, and is mostly of the informative kind, carried in the Polish technical press. There are some 60 Polish technical publications covering a wide field of activities. Advertising is handled by the State Advertising Agency - AGPOL, Ul. Sienkievicza 12, Warsaw. Foreign products may also be advertised in the publications of the Polish Chamber of Foreign Trade.

## POLISH CHAMBER OF FOREIGN TRADE

The Polish Chamber of Foreign Trade is an institution that brings together enterprises conducting international trade.  Its members are foreign trade and international transport enterprises, individual factories producing for export, banks, and enterprises engaged in controlling and inspecting goods, insurance, arbitrage and port services.  The main purpose of the Chamber is to promote and strengthen economic relations with foreign countries.  Its functions are similar to those of the chambers of other socialist countries.

## V.  QUALITY CONTROL AND INSPECTION

Polish FTOs and trade units of enterprises have standardized quality definition by adopting national standards.  If the national norms for any goods do not correspond to the requirements of the world market, a reference is made to the appropriate national standard in the contract, with a reservation allowing for improvement of the quality of the goods in question.

Machinery and equipment are bought and sold mostly according to technical terms usually stipulated by the buyer but, in some cases, by the seller.  The quality of some types of machinery and equipment is measured according to international standards.  If there are no national or industrial quality standards for imported goods, contracts with foreign suppliers are concluded only with the agreement of the chief consumer.  When manufactured consumer goods are imported, the importing organization and the suppliers establish a guarantee period.

Diagnostic apparatus, drugs and medical equipment for which there are no national or industrial standards and which are not on the list of domestically produced medicines may be imported only by the Ministry of Health.

The following institutions are responsible for quality control:

(a)  Ministerstwo Handlu Zagranicznego i Gospodarki Morskiej, Centralny Inspektorat Standartyzacji (CIS), Ul. Stepinksa 9, 00-957 Warsaw, compulsorily controls the quality of all farm products and foodstuffs exported from Poland. It supervises the production of these products at certain stages, issues appropriate instructions and inspects consignments of goods intended for export at enterprises, loading facilities and border stations.  If CIS has doubts about the quality of a consignment to be sent abroad, the goods will be detained.  It also checks that the quality of imported goods corresponds to the standards stipulated in the contract.  CIS activities are mandatory, and therefore it does not accept orders for carrying out quality examination.

(b)  POLCARGO handles quality and quantity control for any goods at the request of Polish and foreign companies and industries;  and

(c)  SUPERVISE effects quality and quantity control on the same basis as POLCARGO.

## VI.  BANKING SYSTEM

The Narodowy Bank Polski (National Bank of Poland) is the bank of issue and the central credit, savings, clearing and foreign exchange bank.  It regulates the circulation of currency, participates in drafting economic plans, fixes foreign exchange rates, supervises foreign currency transactions of other banks and institutions, and extends credit to Polish enterprises.

The Bank Handlowy (Foreign Trade Bank) is the bank most directly involved in foreign trade activities. It supervises, performs and finances the banking operations of Polish FTOs and other enterprises and usually negotiates directly with foreign banks. Its general functions include: financing investment activities of FTOs and other enterprises; settlement of accounts in foreign trade turnover and foreign trade services; and granting foreign exchange credits to units of the socialist sector. The bank is also authorized to grant and receive foreign credits, to secure loans and accept warrants in foreign trade, and to carry out foreign currency operations.

## METHODS AND TERMS OF PAYMENTS

All the usual terms of payments, ranging from cash payment to long-term credit for 8-10 years, are in use. Polish FTOs and other enterprises may insist on credit terms, varying from 90 to 180 days.

Cash transactions are handled on a cash against documents (c.a.d.) basis. The exporter's bank sends the documents to the Bank Handlowy, which pays after receiving them. For imports, FTOs and other enterprises may establish letters of credit with Bank Handlowy, stipulating the usual conditions of shipment. When buying plant and machinery, FTOs and other enterprises usually ask for deferred-payment terms, which may extend up to 10 years. Similarly, when exporting plant and machinery, they also offer deferred-payment credit terms.

## VII. MARKETING LOGISTICS

### SHIPPING

International sea transport passes through Poland's Baltic ports of Gdansk, Gdynia, Szczecin, Świnoujście and Kołobrzeg, which are administered by Port Authorities and provide such services as reloading, trimming and stevedoring, storage, towing, piloting and mooring. In 1979, the number of ships sailing under the Polish flag was 312, with a total capacity of 4,500,000 deadweight tons. Sea cargo is carried by three shipping companies: Polish Ocean Lines (PLO - Polskie Linie Oceaniczne) handles the transport of general cargo on regular lines; Polish Steamship Company (PZM - Polska Żegluga Morska) handles the transport of bulk and liquid cargo (in tankers); and Polish Baltic Steamship Company (PZB - Polska Żegluga Bałtycka) handles transport in small vessels to nearby destinations, as well as ferry services.

Polfracht, the only chartering agent in the country, charters Polish or foreign vessels for transporting bulk cargo on behalf of Polish or foreign shippers. shippers. It also acts as broker between shipper and carrier, and enters into a contract in their name and on their account for transportation of cargo by sea.

There are two maritime agencies, Morska Agencja in Gdynia and Szczecin ports. The agency in Gdynia, which represents more than 90 foreign shipping companies on regular lines, acts as a general representative of shipping interests and provides them with a wide variety of services, such as cargo supervision, claims, legal disputes, arbitration and salvage. The agency in Szczecin services the Szczecin/ Świnoujście port complex, as well as Kołobrzeg port. It services 15 regular lines, 12 of which are Polish and 3 foreign.

Polish United Baltic Corporation (<u>Polska Ziednoczona Korporacja Bałtycka</u>) acts as general agents and port shipbrokers for booking cargo and clearing ships of the United Baltic Corporation, London, which sail weekly on the Poland-United Kingdom route, in co-operation with Polish Ocean Lines.

There are also agencies providing various services for ships calling at Polish ports. These include: Baltona (supplying duty-free articles to ships' crews); Ciech (providing bunker deliveries); Navimor (undertaking repairs, reconstruction and modernization of ships), and Port Service (undertaking clearing, etc., of vessels).

The Polish Register of Shipping (PRS), which has agreements on co-operation and reciprocal representation with similar organizations in several other countries, performs technical supervision of vessels, during both construction and operation. It grants a class to a vessel built under its supervision.

## AIR

The Polish airline, LOT (<u>Polskie Linie Lotnicze</u>), handles both passenger and cargo transport. It is a member of the International Air Transport Association (IATA). LOT offers regular direct flights from Warsaw to a large number of destinations in Western and Eastern Europe, North America, Asia and Africa. Cargo is carried on regular flights or, in the case of large shipments, by means of special chartered planes. Tariffs are adapted to the general conditions and regulations for all the airlines associated with IATA.

## TRANSPORTATION

Next to maritime transport, railways play a significant role in the transportation of freight in Poland's foreign trade. Poland's geographical position at the crossroads of the main west-east north-south trade routes accounts for its large transit transportation. Polish State Railways are members of the socialist countries' railways co-operation organization, OSZD, which has headquarters in Warsaw, as well as of the International Railway Transport Union (UIC) in Bern, the members of which are the railways of the European countries, the Near East and North America.

International road transportation is handled by the PKS enterprise, a member of the International Road Haulage Carriers Association and the International Road Transport Union (IRU). Arranging international road transportation is the responsibility of the international forwarding enterprise, C. Hartwig. PKS transports all types of goods in Polish foreign trade to all countries in Europe, the Near East and North America. C. Hartwig provides forwarding services for foreign and domestic shippers and also takes charge of transit transport through Poland. It has agents throughout the world.

## INSURANCE

Insurance and reinsurance services in Poland are provided by WARTA, which provides cover for goods in sea, land and air transport, as well as during their storage en route.

## VIII.  TRADE DOCUMENTATION AND ARBITRATION

### CONTRACTS

Intra-CMEA trade is governed by the General Terms of CMEA Deliveries.  When trading with non-socialist countries, Polish FTOs apply the general terms of contracts used in world trade.  These contracts will specify the normal standard terms, including force majeure, arbitration, sanctions, guarantees, inspection tests, acceptance of goods, transportation terms, documentation requirements, etc.

### ARBITRATION

The Court of Arbitration was established by the Council of the Polish Chamber of Foreign Trade in 1949.  It is a permanent court of conciliation and is responsible for settling disputes arising from contracts covering the sale, transport and insurance of goods, as well as from all types of commercial activities and services in which at least one of the parties is a person or legal entity residing or having its seat outside Poland.  The Court acts on the basis of regulations passed by the Chamber of Foreign Trade.

### DOCUMENTATION

Since imports are effected by FTOs, the documentation requirements for exporters of each commercial contract are authoritative and definitive in that particular case, irrespective of the value and mode of transport used.  Contracts will specify the documents required (plus the number of copies of each), important points that must be covered by each document, the language(s) acceptable for use in the documents, whether certification and/or legislation may be necessary, any special certificates that may be required for the order in question, plus any regulations that must be met in shipping the goods.  Packing, marking and labelling requirements that must be met will also be specified in the covering contract. Facsimile signatures are not permitted on documents.  The following are the detailed documentation requirements, based on Polish laws and/or regulations:

(a)  Air way bills.  Nine copies on standard IATA forms;

(b)  Bills of lading.  No special requirements;

(c)  Commercial invoices:  Four.  If requested by the importer, they should be certified by the Polish Commercial Counsellor's Office in the exporting country;

(d)  Consular fees.  None;

(e)  Import licence.  Required for all shipments;

(f)  Marking packages.  No special requirements;

(g)  Packing materials.  No special requirements;

(h)  Samples.  Duty-free, if of no commercial value;

(i)  Shipper's export declaration.  Required for all shipments;  and

(j)  Special certificates.  Imports of animals and animal parts and products are subject to restrictions.  Pharmaceuticals must be registered with the Instytut Leków at the Ministry of Health;

(k)  Insurance bills.

Annex

List of some commercial publications of the socialist countries of Eastern Europe

| Name of publication | Publisher | Frequency | Language | Contents |
|---|---|---|---|---|
| **USSR** | | | | |
| Narodnoie Hoziaistvo SSSR (National Economy of the USSR) | Statistics (Publishers) Kirova St., 39, Moscow | Annually – October | Russian | Statistical annual for all branches of industry and the economy |
| Vneshniaia Torgovlia SSSR (Foreign Trade of the USSR) | Finance and Statistics (Publishers) Chernyshevskogo Str.7, Moscow | Annually – November (abroad) obtainable earlier in Moscow | Russian | By country and by product for the two preceding years. Quantity and value of imports and exports of each country is given, using official CMEA classification |
| Vneshniaia Torgovlia (Foreign Trade) | Ministry of Foreign Trade of the USSR | Monthly | Russian English French German Spanish | Feature articles on foreign trade. Selected statistics published in each edition. The August issue has complete import-export statistics by country for the two preceding years |
| **BULGARIA** | | | | |
| Bulgarian Foreign Trade | Bulgarian Chamber of Commerce Ila Stamboliiski Blivd., Sofia | Every two months | English French Spanish Russian German | Informative articles on Bulgarian foreign trade institutions and developments |

| Name of publication | Publisher | Frequency | Language | Contents |
|---|---|---|---|---|
| Foreign Trade of the People's Republic of Bulgaria | State Information Board, Sofia | Annually | English | Statistics on exports and imports, in both absolute and relative terms. Includes exports and imports of means of production, consumer, industrial and agricultural goods. Exports and imports, are classified by type of transport, country, regional groups of countries, and commodity |
| Foreign Trade Reference Book | Bulgarian Chamber of Commerce | | English | Brief survey of the historical development of foreign trade and key institutions dealing with foreign trade |
| Statisticheski Esegodnik narodnoi Republiki Bulgar (Statistical Yearbook of the People's Republic of Bulgaria) | Central Statistical Office to the Council | Annually | Russian English | Statistical annual of all sectors of the economy |
| Economic News from Bulgaria | Chamber of Commerce, Sofia | Monthly | English French German | Current information of foreign trade, trade agreements, new products, etc. |
| Statistics of Internal Trade | State Information Board, Sofia | Annually | English | |

| Name of publication | Publisher | Frequency | Language | Contents |
|---|---|---|---|---|
| Statistics of Investment | State Information Board, Sofia | Annually | English | Detailed summary of foreign trade. Lists all major trade partners by broad product classification for 7 years - 1939, 1950, 1955, 1960, 1965, 1967 and 1968 |
| 25 Years of Bulgarian Foreign Trade Statistical Data 1939-68 | Ministry of Foreign Trade, Sofia - 1969 | | Bulgarian English French | |
| CZECHOSLOVAKIA | | | | |
| Czechoslovakia Statistical Abstract | Orbis Prague Vihohradska | Annually | English German Russian | Includes 7 pages of fine print data on output by individual product |
| Statistiks Recenka ČSSR (Statistical Yearbook) | Federal Statistical Office, Prague | Annually - in summer for previous year | Czechoslovak with English summaries | A summary statistical survey of all economic sectors, administration and culture. Contains national, regional and international data |
| Facts on Czechoslovak Foreign Trade | Rapid/Chamber of Commerce, 13 Ul. 28 rijina, Prague 1 | Annually - in August/September for previous year | English French | Includes foreign trade statistics, data on relevant governmental organizations, FTOs, foreign trade legislation, commodity and territorial structure of foreign trade and Czechoslovak participation in international organizations |

| Name of publication | Publisher | Frequency | Language | Contents |
|---|---|---|---|---|
| **GERMAN DEMOCRATIC REPUBLIC** | | | | |
| Die Wirtschaft | Verlag Die Wirtschaft Berlin | Monthly | German | Articles frequently cover foreign trade, economic industrial sectors and include detailed trade statistics |
| Statistisches Jahrbuch (Statistical Yearbook) | State Central Administration for Statistics, State Publishers, Berlin | Annually - in autumn | German with English translation of the terms used in the tables | Historical investment product import data. Output by individual product. Exports and imports of the leading industrial branches are listed in greater detail according to value, but not according to destination of source |
| Statistische Praxis | Central Statistical Office, Berlin | Monthly | German | Periodically includes comprehensive statistics for an economic or industrial sector |
| **HUNGARY** | | | | |
| Kulkereskedelmi Ertesito | Ministry of Foreign Trade, Budapest | Monthly | Hungarian English Russian | Selected issues cover specialized subjects |
| Statistical Pocket-book of Hungary | Hungarian Central Statistical Office, Budapest | Annually - July/August | English | Statistical annual for all economic sectors, including national income and investments, industry, agriculture, transport and communications, foreign and domestic trade, tourism, employment, etc. Includes vital statistics |

| Name of publication | Publisher | Frequency | Language | Contents |
|---|---|---|---|---|
| Statistical Yearbook | Hungarian Central Statistical Office Budapest | Annually – in summer for previous year | Hungarian English | Complete statistical annual for all sectors of the economy. Includes vital statistics, historical investment, production and import data by output of individual product |
| Statistikal Havi Lizlemenyek (Monthly Bulletin of Statistics) | Hungarian Central Statistical Office Budapest | Monthly | Hungarian English | Production data and vital statistics. Also information concerning imports and exports of certain commodities |
| **POLAND** | | | | |
| Concise Statistical Yearbook of Poland | Central Statistical Office, Warsaw | Annually – in February for previous year | Polish English French Russian | Statistical annual for all sectors of the economy – industry, agriculture, trade – and for all aspects of life in Poland |
| Polish Economic Survey | Polish Press Agency Trebacka, 4, Warsaw 1 | Fortnightly | Polish English | Summarizes latest trade agreements, commercial transactions, product and economic measures for both home and foreign use |
| Rocznik Statystyczny (Statistical Yearbook) | Central Statistical Office, Warsaw | Annually – in summer | Polish | Detailed data on investment, production and imports, including comparative data for previous year |
| Rocznik Statystyczny Handlu Zagranicynego (Foreign Trade Statistics) | Central Statistical Office, Warsaw | Annually | Polish | Gives total trade by industrial sector, by product for many items and by country. Detailed trade statistics |